MW00575058

The Lapsley Saga

The Lapsley Saga

Psalm 115:1

Winifred K. and Lachlan C. Vass III

Winifred K. and Lachlan C. Vass

PROVIDENCE HOUSE PUBLISHERS
Franklin, Tennessee

01   00   99   98   97   5   4   3   2   1

Library of Congress Catalog Card Number: 96–72388

ISBN: 1–57736–023–0

Cover by Bozeman Design

PROVIDENCE HOUSE PUBLISHERS
238 Seaboard Lane • Franklin, Tennessee 37067
800-321-5692

To Our Fathers

The Reverend Lachlan Cumming Vass II
Missionary in the Congo Free State, 1898–1910
Beloved Pastor of Churches in Tennessee, Georgia, and
Mississippi, 1910–1948

Doctor Eugene Roland Kellersberger
Medical Missionary in the Belgian Congo, 1916–1940
General Secretary of the American Leprosy Missions, Inc.,
1940–1953

Contents

Acknowledgments

With heartfelt appreciation, the authors of this book acknowledge the contributions made to its publication by the following:

To Louise England (Mrs. Albert England) for her scholarly proofreading of the entire manuscript and for the excellent, helpful suggestions she made.

To Andre Lederer of the Catholic University of Louvain, member of the Royal Academy of Overseas Sciences, for permission to reproduce the map of the Congo River System, printed in his book, *Histoire de la Navigation au Congo*, Musée Royal de l'Afrique Centrale, Tervuren, Belgique, Annales Serie IN-8, Sciences Historiques No. 2, 1965.

To Ph. Marechal, Chef de Section Musée Royal de l'Afrique Centrale, Tervuren, Belgique, for permission to reproduce the photographs of two of the steamers on which the Reverend Samuel N. Lapsley traveled: Grenfell's *Peace* and the state steamer *Florida*.

To Rev. Alastair Scougal, chaplain, International Student Ministries of the United Protestant Church of Belgium in Brussels,

Belgium, for implementing our many requests to him for historical materials relating to the Congo Free State and the Belgian Congo.

To the staff of the Department of History, Montreat, North Carolina, Presbyterian Church (U.S.A.), for so willingly making available to us their resources of information on the American Presbyterian Congo Mission, including the Minutes and Files of the Executive Committee of Foreign Missions of the Presbyterian Church (U.S.), issues of denominational publications of the 1890s and early 1900s, and the Lapsley, Morrison, and Vass Collections.

We are particularly grateful for the ready personal assistance of Robert Benedetto, former deputy director of the Department of History, Montreat, North Carolina; of William Bynum, assistant director for reference; of Diana Ruby-Sanderson, special collections archivist; and of John Walker, technical services/reference librarian.

To Helen Isanuzzi of the Department of History, Philadelphia, Pennsylvania, for her help with photographs of the *Lapsley*.

To Rev. Terry Newland, pastor of the Central Presbyterian Church of Anniston, Alabama, and to Catherine Bowling, who researched that church's records for information on Rev. Samuel N. Lapsley and his family.

To Mrs. Glenn Murray, our thanks for pictures of Lapsley's grave and the graveyard near Matadi.

To Rev. Howard D. Cameron for finding the long-missing *Lapsley* shipyard job plaque and obtaining information from the *Lapsley's* builders, Simons-Lobnitz, Ltd.

To all those who contributed memories of being aboard the *Lapsley*, our grateful thanks: Anne Boyd Cleveland Crane, Louise Crane, Elizabeth McKee Gerding, Ruth Smith Gilmer, Dorothy Longenecker Hopper, Alice Longenecker, Rev. Charles McKee, Anne Wilds McLean, Dr. John Knox Miller, "Sanky" Stegall Norwood, and Georgia McKay Watt.

To Eleanora Anderson Worth and her husband, William C. Worth, for the picture of the *Lapsley* tied to the riverbank, taken by her father, Dr. Vernon A. Anderson.

To Frances Ogden Foreman, for her very special personal contribution of firsthand family information on Rev. Samuel N.

Lapsley, who was her great uncle. Mrs. Foreman's mother lived in Lapsley's boyhood home throughout school sessions of her childhood years; it was she who recalled Lapsley's mother's daily prayer for her family.

To Dr. Kenneth J. Foreman Jr. for his perceptive critique of the manuscript in preparation and particularly for his assistance in writing the conclusion, which tells of his own search for any remains of the *Samuel N. Lapsley*.

To Mrs. Eula B. Oprendek for her continued interest and loving encouragement during the years of preparation of this manuscript.

Above all, to our Lord Jesus Christ, for the rare privilege of growing up with the heritage of parents who are written about in this book. We thank God for vivid memories of the years in which we lived and worked at Luebo, for having walked the decks of the mission steamer and for having known personally most of those who move and speak in this book. Ours has been a unique opportunity to observe and record the events related in THE LAPSLEY SAGA.

Foreword: The Zaire River System

Africa's great tropical heart is ruled by the majestic colossus of the Zaire River system. Alternately treacherously constricted or calmly, broadly navigable, it is a river personality totally distinct from all other river personalities of the world.

The Zaire is unique in that it straddles the equator, crossing it twice, first from the south and then from the north, as it pursues its grand, arching 2,900 mile-long sweep from towering mountain sources to a cavernous ocean mouth. Also in a category of its own because of its magnitude, the river covers a drainage area of 1,425,000 square miles and has 8500 miles of navigable waterways dotted with some 4000 islands. Its hydroelectric power potential is equal to that of all the rivers of the United States combined. These unusual geographical and topographical features radically shaped the history of its exploration.[1]

Modern writers have called the Zaire "the world's most dramatic river"[2] and "a Titan with a toehold in the sea."[3] Joseph Conrad called it "an immense snake uncoiled, with its head in the sea and its tail lost in the depths of the land." He referred to the river world of crowding undergrowth, deep, dark water, and eerie silence as "the stillness of an implacable force brooding over an inscrutable intention."[4]

Henry M. Stanley, who knew the river best, wrote,

> We did not believe that there was any end to that great river . . . the hateful, murderous river now so broad and proud and majestically calm, as though it had not bereft me of a friend and many faithful souls, and as though we had never heard it rage and whiten with fury and mock the thunder! What a hypocritical river![5]

This "double-saddle" position of the Zaire astride the equator causes alternating rainy seasons, one in the northern hemisphere and one in the southern, giving the river two annual flood stages in May and November. Where the rivers coming from opposite sides of the equator meet, the difference in low, dry-season and rainy, flood-stage water levels creates deadly maelstroms in which human lives are often lost.

The first 1,300 miles of the Upper Zaire, beginning in Malawi with the Chambezi, flow due north, fed by various rivers draining off the highlands and mountain ranges that form the western side of the Great Rift Valley. These rivers join to form the Lualaba, which continues to flow north-northwest toward the equator. At Kisangani the Lualaba becomes the Zaire and passes through a narrow gorge called "The Gate of Hell." From there it broadens and turns westward. Stanley Falls, a series of seven cataracts, marks the end of the Upper Zaire and the beginning of the truly remarkable "Channel," a wide, 980-mile-long stretch of beautifully navigable waters, unbroken by rapids. Then again, the river coils northward, crossing the equator to its most northerly point. Swerving in a southwesterly direction some 250 miles lower, it flows around slender islands 30 and 50 miles long! Now 9 miles wide, it courses another 125 miles through a stretch totally free of islands. The river is then joined from the south by its most important tributary, the Kasai, and at Kwamouth thunders through a chasm between the hills only 700 yards wide.

Over the entire 980 miles from Stanley Falls, the elevation of the river drops only 500 feet!

The lower section of the Zaire begins at Stanley Pool (Malebo) where it creates a river-lake 20 miles long and 14 miles wide. At the western end of the Pool is the neighboring capital of Congo/Brazzaville. To the south, only 300 yards above the first cataract of Livingston Falls, Kinshasa, the capital of Zaire, begins its urban sprawl of three million people.

With the speed of some 600 feet a minute and a roar heard miles away, the Zaire hurls itself over the continental shelf down to sea level. For 215 miles the combined waters of the rivers of Zaire plunge down 800 feet, over a series of thirty rapids, through the twisted, tortured terrain of the Crystal Mountains. The lowest rapid is just above Matadi (Rocks), the river port at the terminus of oceangoing navigation. The Zaire below Matadi is only a half-mile wide, forming Hell's Caldron, which has deadly, swirling whirlpools, and currents of from four to eight knots.

At Banana the mammoth river pours through a seven-mile-wide mouth into the Atlantic Ocean. A tremendous canyon has been gouged deep into the ocean floor by the formidable force of a water volume calculated at 1,200,000 cubic feet or more per second. Extending a hundred miles out to sea, this canyon has had depths sounded as much as 4000 feet below ocean-floor level. Three hundred miles out to sea the red-brown soil-laden waters of the Zaire are clearly differentiated from blue ocean waters.

Even the names of the river have an interesting linguistic history. During the colonial era, 1880–1960, it was called "The Congo," named for the large and powerful ethnic group through whose lands the river flows into the Atlantic Ocean. This was its designation during the years in which the events in this book took place and were recorded.

In 1971, General Mobutu Sese Suko decreed that the river, the nation, and its currency were all henceforth to be called "Zaire." The river's ancient traditional Bantu name was "Zaidi," which is derived from the root of the verb "to eat," because "it is the great river that *eats up* or *swallows* all other rivers." "Zaidi" is a common Bantu personal name; a member of Stanley's caravan was named

"Zaidi." Early Portuguese explorers, inquiring what the river was called, corrupted the pronunciation to "Zaire," an odd trick to play on a people who do not even have an "r" in their alphabet![6]

The Zaire River is historically unique because it is the only major river of the world to be first fully explored from its *source* end down to the ocean. The mouth of the river was discovered and claimed in 1482 by Diego Cam, with no attempt to explore its inland reaches. In 1485 Cam returned with three caravels, only to discover that the broad, inviting estuary was totally deceptive as an entryway into the African continent. At the swirling edge of Hell's Caldron, the Portuguese explorer was forced to turn his violently tossing ship about and return to sea. On his disappointed way downstream, some fifty yards from the rocky peninsula called Fishermen's Caves, just below the Caldron, he inscribed the Portuguese cross, his name, and the date 1485 under a large rock projection beneath an overhanging cliff, where it still may be seen today. The exploration of the upper Zaire beyond the great natural barrier had to wait for another four hundred years. It was Henry Morton Stanley who, in 1876, painfully traced the perverse river from its small source on the upland plateau all the way down to the Atlantic Ocean, taking 999 days to complete the arduous journey.[7]

It was upon the waters of various parts of this challenging Zaire River system that the events of THE LAPSLEY SAGA occurred. The gargantuan river itself is the main character, providing the fluid, constantly moving setting for the Lilliputian figures silhouetted against its silver surface: two missionaries, two churning paddle wheel steamers, six mission captains, and several commercial river transport pilots.

In 1891 the Reverend Samuel N. Lapsley and his African-American associate, the Reverend William H. Sheppard, journeyed up the Zaire River and its most important tributary, the Kasai. This is the river that drains the vast, magnificent upland heart of the

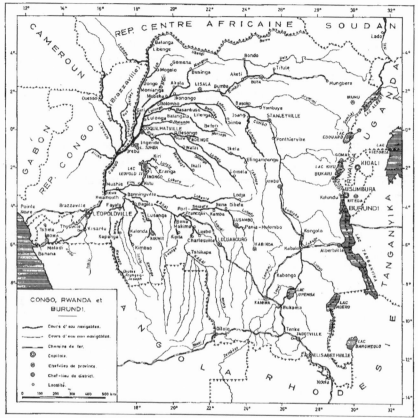

System of Navigable Waterways of the Belgian Congo (1908–1960). Courtesy—Andre Lederer, Histoire de la Navigation au Congo, Musée Royale de l'Afrique Centrale (1915), Tervuren, Belgique.

continent, cradled within the giant, encircling curve of the mother river. At the headwaters of navigation, the confluence of the Lulua and Luebo Rivers, Lapsley and Sheppard established Luebo mission station and founded the American Presbyterian Congo Mission (1892–1959). After only two brief years, Lapsley died of blackwater fever. The flaming flare of his life launched the spray-soaked navigational careers of the two mission paddle wheelers named for him.

The first *Samuel N. Lapsley*, like the life of the man for whom it was named, functioned only briefly and ended tragically when it capsized at Kwamouth with a great loss of life. But the busy, adventurous, twenty-five-year-long mission-service career of the sturdy second *Samuel N. Lapsley* was made possible by the initial sacrifice of that pioneer missionary's life, as well as the failure of the first, frail "trial" vessel from which much was learned about the lethal power of the deceptive brooding river.

Other "actors" in this river drama are the Reverend Lachlan C. Vass Jr., fresh from theological seminary, who assembled both of the vessels at Stanley Pool and captained them. W. B. Scott, the Reverend A. C. McKinnon, Joseph Daumery, the Reverend Hugh Wilds, and Franklin Watt also served at the helm until the Great Depression forced the sale in 1930 of the beloved mission steamer. Purchased by a commercial agent, the *Lapsley* enjoyed a second thirty-year-long career as a transportation vessel and "floating store."

Personal letters, diaries, and records written by the Reverend Lachlan C. Vass Jr. are the main sources of information for THE LAPSLEY SAGA.

Notes

1. Peter Forbath, *The River Congo* (New York: Harper & Row, 1977), 3–18.

2. Ibid.

3. John J. Putnam and Eliot Elisofom, "Yesterday's Congo, Today's Zaire," *National Geographic*, vol. 143, no. 3 (March 1973): 398–432.

4. Joseph Conrad, *Heart of Darkness* (Englewood, NJ: Prentice-Hall, Inc., 1960), 27–29, 47–48.

5. Henry M. Stanley, *In Darkest Africa* (New York: Charles Scribner's Sons, 1890), 88.

6. Robert Caputo, "Zaire River, Lifeline of a Nation," *National Geographic*, vol. 180, no. 5 (November 1991): 10–11.

7. Guide de la Section de *L'Etat Independant du Congo a l'Exposition, Bruxelles-Teruvuren en 1897*, Bruxelles, Imprimerie Veuve Monnom, 32, rue de l'Industrie (Regions Maritime-Kasai), 4–196.

Additional Sources

Gunther, John. *Inside Africa*. New York: Harper & Brothers, 1953 (Congo River, 649–50, 654–55, 692).

Kaplan, Irving, ed. *Zaire, A Country Study*, Foreign Area Studies, The American University. Research completed May 1978. (Superintendent of Documents, U.S. Government Printing Office, Washington, D.C., 20402.) ("Zaire River," xv, 12, 108, 123, 135, 229, 234–35, 237).

Lederer, Andre. *Histoire de la Navigation au Congo*. Musée Royal de l'Afrique Centrale, Tervuren, Belgique, Annales, Serie IN-8, Sciences Historiques, no. 2, 1965 (Zaire River, 7–8, 33, 359).

Michiels, A. et N. Laude. *Notre Colonie*, Edition Universelle S.A., 90, rue Royale, Bruxelles, 30–43.

Traveler's Guide to the Belgian Congo and Ruanda-Urundi, Second Edition, 1956. Published by the Tourist Bureau for the Belgian Congo and Ruanda-Urundi, III Directorate, Information and Public Relations Bureau, 28, Potterie, Brussels, Belgium, 68–72.

Tuckey, J. K. *Narrative of an Expedition to Explore the River Zaire, Usually Called the Congo*, London, 1818.

Part I

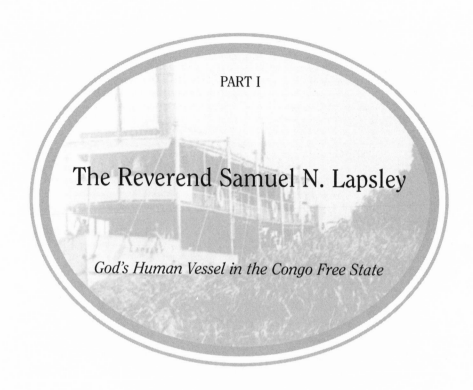

PART I

The Reverend Samuel N. Lapsley

God's Human Vessel in the Congo Free State

The Making of the Missionary
April 14, 1866–February 25, 1890

BAREFOOTED, FAIR HAIR TOUSLED BY THE WIND, LITTLE Sam Lapsley was often seen with his black playmates, happily roaming the wide fields and piney woods of his family's four-hundred-acre country home in Alabama. Letters he wrote in later years recalled with wistful nostalgia the innocent fun they had splashing in Big Mulberry Creek, their favorite swimming hole, and the fascinating, leisurely chats with his beloved old ex-slave friend, Uncle Josh. "I do like the black folks very much!" he wrote to his brother, James, from his Congo mission station. Those early years spent in the American deep South established the warm, accepting attitude that characterized the missionary to Africa.[1]

3

The Reverend Samuel Norvell Lapsley when he sailed for the Congo Free State on February 25, 1890. Courtesy—Department of History, PCUSA, Montreat, North Carolina.

Samuel Norvell Lapsley was born in Selma, Alabama, on April 14, 1866, to Judge James Woods Lapsley and his wife, Sara E. Pratt Lapsley. Both of Sam's parents were children of Presbyterian ministers. His father was at one time the law partner of Senator John Tyler Morgan of Alabama. An active elder and lay evangelist, Judge Lapsley was the very first layman to be elected moderator of the General Assembly of the Presbyterian Church in the United States. His mother's often repeated prayer at daily family worship was: "Lord, separate this family for Thy service!" Three of the sons became ministers and two daughters were wives of ministers. So, it is evident that the prayers were answered.[2]

Young Sam joined the Church on April 16, 1876, a serious, confident ten year old, deeply aware of the important step he was taking. When he was twelve, he began to assist his great aunt, Mrs. Elsie M. Kay, in the Sunday school of the small Vine Hill Church, built for the field-workers and their families by Judge Lapsley and his brothers. His aunt lovingly recalled:

> ... how the earnest little fellow gravely carried on his duties as Sunday School Superintendent. I well remember the first meeting when Sam had to open the school with prayer and say a few words to the crowd that filled the church. He was badly frightened and came near breaking down once, but he looked toward me and caught my eye and went on and got through nicely.

The pastor of the local African-American Baptist church, also attended by the field-workers, often remained after the meeting to discuss some doctrinal point he wished to bring up in a sermon. Mrs. Kay wrote, "I remember Sam's sedate manner as, pacing up and down or standing before William, he would say, 'But, Uncle William, what does Paul say about that?' And he then would quote to him the Scripture."[3]

In 1881, at the age of fifteen Sam Lapsley entered the University of Alabama as a sophomore, graduating with honors in 1884. His teacher, Dr. James A. Waddell, who helped him prepare for college, said he was "the most brilliant pupil he had ever had." During his senior year and the year following his graduation, he was an assistant professor. He was also cadet captain of the Corps of University of Alabama Cadets, a "crack" military drill team that won first prize in competitive drill at the 1885 New Orleans Exposition.[4]

The many fine qualities of Sam Lapsley's maturing character were now evident. He had a delightful sense of humor and a rare gift for making friends. Both genial and congenial, he was a born leader, brilliantly gifted intellectually. He was also musically talented; he played the old "pump organ" as a boy for Vine Hill Sunday School, and, as a seminary student, played and led the singing in gospel tent meetings. His African diary contains some of the native songs he heard, their unique syncopated rhythm carefully captured in his detailed handwritten musical notations. Above all, he was temperamentally and spiritually fitted for the special pioneer task to which his Master called him. It was the *physical* "earthen vessel" that was to break under the vicious onslaught of tropical disease!

Lapsley's seminary training included one year (1885–1886) at Union Presbyterian Theological Seminary in Richmond, Virginia, and two years (1887–1889) at McCormick Theological Seminary in Chicago. Between his first and middle years, the ministerial student gained pastoral experience in the Alabama towns of Decatur, Hartsell, Somerville, and Fairview, and also at the Second Presbyterian Church of Birmingham, where he worked for several months with the famous "Brother Bryan."

His decision to transfer to McCormick was prompted by his determination to experience Chicago's inner city, as well as his

FORM OF LICENSURE.

At *Livingston Ala.* the *16th* day of *April 1867*
the Presbytery of *Tuskaloosa* having received
Testimonials in favor of *Samuel N. Lapsley*
of his having gone through a regular course of Literature; of his
good moral character; and of his being in the communion of the
Church; proceeded to take the usual parts of trial for his licensure: and he having given satisfaction as to his accomplishments
in Literature; as to his experimental acquaintance with Religion;
and as to his proficiency in Divinity and other studies; the Presbytery did, and hereby do, express their approbation of all these
parts of trial: and he having adopted the Confession of Faith
of this Church, and satisfactorily answered the questions appointed
to be put to Candidates to be licensed; the Presbytery did, and
hereby do license him, the said *Samuel N. Lapsley*
to preach the Gospel of Christ, as a Probationer for the Holy
Ministry, within the bounds of this Presbytery, or wherever else
he shall be orderly called.

ATTEST: *J. G. Praigg*

*Stated Clerk of the Presbytery of
Tuskaloosa.*

Samuel Lapsley's "Form of Licensure" as an ordained minister of the Presbyterian
Church, U.S. Courtesy—Department of History, PCUSA, Montreat, North Carolina.

familiar, rural deep South. While there, he helped start the Chicago City Mission which later became the Olivet Presbyterian Church.[5]

After his graduation in 1889, Lapsley went to Anniston, Alabama, where his family had moved. He immediately became involved in the Glen Addie Mission in the southwestern part of the city, which later became the Anniston Third Church. He also established another mission outpost near the homes of the ore washers of the Woodstock Iron Company for the families of the factory workers living in that district. A deep impression was made on the Washertown Mission's congregation as their young minister ate and slept in their homes, sharing their daily struggles and problems.[6]

In 1889 the General Assembly of the Presbyterian Church in the United States voted to begin mission work in Africa. Lapsley immediately applied to the Executive Committee of Foreign Missions and was accepted and placed under appointment. He was only twenty-three years old![7]

The Journey with No Return Begins
February 26, 1890–May 9, 1890

Lapsley's future coworker, William Sheppard, was a young African-American minister from Waynesboro, Virginia. The idea of being a missionary to Africa had been planted in his mind very early in his childhood by a Mrs. Ann Bruce, who said to him, "William, I pray for you, and hope that some day you may go to Africa as a missionary." A graduate of Hampton Institute in Virginia and Tuscaloosa Theological Institute in Alabama, he had held successful pastorates in Montgomery, Alabama, and Atlanta, Georgia, and had been waiting for several years for an overseas assignment in Africa from the Presbyterian Church in the United States.[8]

The cofounders of the American Presbyterian Congo Mission met for the first time in the offices of the Executive Committee of Foreign Missions in Nashville, Tennessee. The final instructions of the committee to the two appointees were that they were to work in every way as "coequals."

The Reverend William Henry Sheppard. Courtesy—Department of History, PCUSA, Montreat, North Carolina.

On Wednesday, February 26, 1890, they sailed from New York on the SS *Adriatic*. Lapsley's parents made the trip to New York with their son. As they watched the two departing missionaries mount the gangplank, a mother's loud, tear-choked, brave cry was suddenly heard by all gathered to watch the vessel's departure: "Sheppard, take care of Sam!"[9]

From his lonely cabin at sea that night, Lapsley wrote to his parents:

> I felt as I never had in my life, when I saw you walk out of sight in the great shed. I thought I saw you again on the Battery; waved, ran, tried to see better, but lost you. I didn't know how much I loved you till today. I want a chance again to show you both how much, but I shall try to honor you by being a good man, and filling the place God has put me in, as you have shown me how.

> About twelve miles out, the pilot dropped off and rowed over to the pilot yacht, leaving us to the light-house above the sun by day, the moon and stars by night. I thought my piloting henceforth must be from the Light above. Do you remember, Mamma, we sang, "Pilot Me" at Mr. Moody's meeting? Well, I must find Sheppard for prayers, and say good night for this first day's journey. Your loving son, Sam.

Providentially, also aboard the *Adriatic* for this voyage was an influential London Presbyterian, Mr. Robert Whyte, "a man of great spirituality, a warehouseman and supplier of fancy goods and many other things." The happy, congenial meeting of this successful businessman with the two missionaries began a warm, personal friendship and many years of dedicated assistance to their successors on the field. At the first opportunity, they went to the great four-story building in the heart of London housing Whyte, Ridsdale and Company. Though Mr. Whyte's business was wholesale, he gladly assisted the two missionaries with all the supplies they needed for their work. Highlights of their stay in London were attendance at a meeting of North London Presbytery and an emotional visit to the grave of David Livingstone in Westminster Abbey.[10]

Audience with King Leopold II of Belgium

In 1890 most people still believed that King Leopold II of Belgium was engaged in a great humanitarian crusade in Central Africa. An audience with this monarch was arranged for Lapsley by Henry Sanford, the United States minister to Belgium. Senate Majority Leader John Tyler Morgan had requested him to do all in his power to help launch the new mission.

On March 23, having crossed the English Channel to Belgium, Sam wrote the following from the English Hotel, 44 Rue de Brabant, in Brussels:

> General Sanford has been very kind indeed. He is a zealous Congo man, not a visionary, for he has large interests there. He treats me as if I were on his business; directs all my movements, takes me to see everybody of importance to me, and claims from them in his own and General Morgan's name their good offices for me. He is quite free in his suggestions to me: "If you go to the king, you must have a top hat." So I proceeded to have a tall silk hat, reflecting that Nehemiah would doubtless have had one, and a swallow-tail coat too.

As my interview was to be in the morning, I deferred the dress-coat until my purse is more replete with shekels.

I wore Gus Hall's shoes, Birmingham pants, Chicago coat, "Famous" collar, Brussels hat, Rogers, Peet & Co.'s gloves (you bought them) and cravat of sister Gene's make. Be sure to tell her.

I was ushered into the *Polais* [sic] *Du Roi*, relieved of my overcoat and umbrella by half a dozen liveried attendants, and directed to the great stair and up to the anteroom. There a decorated official received me, and found enough English to let me know I had five minutes to wait, my time was 11:45. By the way, I was terribly scared by this gentleman. He was so much gilded (and so was the room) that I thought I was in the royal presence. He made things worse by two profound bows, before he opened his lips, his heels cracked together, and his spurs rattled smartly.

After about ten minutes it seemed, my courage came back. I was ushered into another great room, and heard a kind voice from the middle of it, "Good Morning!" I was reas-, sured, and after a respectful bow, I advanced and took the hand extended to me. The king said, "You asked to see me?" I told him my business, whom I represented, the Presbyterian body in the United States, what I meant to do, and our plan of working with combined white and black personnel.

He warned me of the entire rudeness of the country, commended our plan of beginning on a small scale, until the tide comes in, on the completion of the railways, then enter on that tide. "The Congo has a future," he said. "I cannot believe that God made that great river with its many branches all through the land, for any lower purpose."

About my location, he recommended the Kasai saying, "I would advise you not to go to the Ubangi yet; we cannot protect you, if you go so far from our stations."

The king asked my age, and said he was glad I had begun the work of Christ so soon. I quite forgot he was a Catholic or a

king, when he spoke with so much apparent sympathy of my
mission. After half an hour's talk, he asked me if I wanted to
speak with him of anything else. He said that he was warmly
interested in my mission, and was glad to see a young man
show "so much courage, enterprise and Christian pluck."

King Leopold is tall, erect and slender, a man, I should say,
forty-seven years of age—no, not that much! His hair is
rather thin and gray, his beard long and fine, turning a little
gray. His eyes are soft and clear, blue, I think. His expression
is very kind, and his voice matches it. He wore a dark green
military frock coat, epaulets and sword, with no star or
decoration whatever. His manner is both bright and gentle,
and his English is full, ready and expressive. I may be
mistaken in my description; I was of course highly strung in
such a presence.

I wonder at his kindness and freeness in talking with me,
and questioning me, for I was not well-dressed nor courtly
in manner, and worst, I had no special business with him. I
wonder now how God has so changed the times that a
Catholic king, successor to Philip II, should talk about
Foreign Missions to an American boy and a Presbyterian![11]

Lapsley and Sheppard returned immediately to London for
two final weeks of preparation and procuring needed supplies.

First Impressions of Lower Congo
May 10, 1890–June 16, 1890

April 18, 1890, the two missionaries sailed from Rotterdam,
Holland, on a Dutch trading vessel, the *Afrikaan*.[12] The lighthouse
on Shark's Point, "the hooked promontory that forms the southern
lip of the mouth of the Congo" River where it flows into the
Atlantic, came into view late in the evening of May 9. Daylight
revealed their first picture-postcard view of the port of Banana.
Long, white-walled buildings could be seen, set among groves of
towering palms, surrounded by tropical *flamboyantes* and shrubs.

With excitement Lapsley watched a rowboat come alongside, manned with a crew of African oarsmen. It made him feel right at home to see them, "muscular, active, rather slight than big," with faces he liked to observe, similar to those of his old friends back on his father's plantation!

During their first weeks in Lower Congo, Sheppard and Lapsley took advantage of every opportunity to visit the stations established in that area and to learn as much as they could from those already experienced in carrying on mission work. At that time mission activity, both Catholic and Protestant, was mostly concentrated in the Lower Congo, below the rapids of the Congo River.

Where the river tumbles precipitously from the high inland plateau down over the continental shelf to sea level, there is a series of thirty-two falls stretching for 230 miles. This is the tremendous geographical barrier that blocked any further exploration by Prince Henry the Navigator's sailors in 1482 when their caravels sailed as far up the river as possible. The Portuguese Cross cut into the cliff just below the boiling river caldron at Matadi marks the point 86 miles from the ocean, at which his sailors admitted defeat by the great river and turned back to sea.

The extreme physical demands of overland travel on foot around the rapids presented a formidable hurdle to inland penetration for state agents, commercial personnel, and missionaries. Not only did travelers have to traverse the rocky terrain in suffocating tropical heat, but every pound of equipment and provision had to be carried on the backs and heads of sweating native carriers, often unwilling to perform such arduous labor. Few men had the pluck and stamina to pay the price for penetration into Congo's heartland of the Upper Congo.

Lapsley's diary records his first impressions and events of the first visits made to nearby posts. On May 9, 1890, he wrote that they traveled in

> . . . a long, narrow canoe, dug out of a large hardwood tree. It was pleasant to hear the paddlers sing as they rowed us along. The "stroke," a fine looking fellow, took the verse and the rest joined heartily in the refrain. The words were simple

sounding and musical; the syllables are so many and quick
that the rhythm is marked and carries you along. It is
complicated with a half-concealed melody.[13]

The first missionary visited was Miss Kildare, Bishop Taylor's
lone lady missionary. Lapsley wrote:

> She is a genuine heroine, full of faith and courage. Her
> material surroundings are pleasant enough. She lives in a
> corrugated iron house, built high enough for a good room
> beneath, with a cool porch in front, a clean, nice yard on one
> side of the house, and a great, thick-growing baobab or
> calabash tree, seven feet in diameter, on the other. Beyond
> the mission station was the native village, where we saw our
> first live African King, his royal highness, Domgele,
> imposing, deliberate, wrapped in a toga like a Roman
> senator, and walking with a royal reed studded with brass
> nail heads. He knew a shilling when we gave him one, and
> sent his Prime Minister for a present in return which
> consisted of three eggs.

A discovery made by Lapsley that day was the way in which
the Congo natives discriminated between the missionary and
other white men. Canny perceivers of human character as it really
is, they were already keenly aware of the differences:

> . . . since Stanley, the State officials, and even the white
> settlement here is called "Bula Matadi." This was Stanley's
> native name which means "breaker-of-rocks," from his
> road-making achievements. The word for "white man" is
> *Mundele*; the word for "missionary" is *Mundele-Nzambi*,
> "God's white man," or sometimes, *Nganga-Nzambi*, "God's
> medicine man." If a party of white men approaches a lower
> Congo village, the cry goes around:
>
> "Who is coming?"
> "*Mundele!*"
> "What *Mundele*?"
> "'*Mundele-Nzambi!*"

> Then out all come to welcome and talk to the travelers. But
> if the answer is "*Weh! Bula Matadi!*" then it's "Sh-sh," and
> whiz! they all go hiding into the tall grass.[14]

Lapsley's description of the banks of the Congo River is vivid:

> The banks of the great river are most interesting. Sometimes
> there is full, deep dark forest, mangrove or large trees with
> creepers and undergrowth, dense and impenetrable. Or
> there is lighter, more oriental growth, the feather-duster
> palm, high as a pine tree, against a rich forest hill, with low,
> fern-like palms lining the waterside. Here and there is a
> strip of beach, then broad, open land against the clear, tea-
> colored water, lined with six-foot-high water-grass which is
> a beautiful green. Finally, both banks converge to the deep
> Congo gorge from Boma to the falls.[15]

After a short stop at Boma, the head government post of the
Congo Free State at that time, the two Presbyterian missionaries
proceeded upriver to a station of the English Baptist Missionary
Society, called Underhill, in the Kikongo language, *Tunduwa*. It is
located on the south bank of the Congo, thirty miles above Boma at
the point in the river where Lapsley remarked: "It gets a current in
the midstream like a mill tail, forming an awful whirlpool!" Just
around this promontory is Matadi ("Rocks"), the head of navigation
and starting point of the Congo Railway around the rapids to Stanley
Pool. Only two miles of this project had been completed at that time.

During their month's sojourn at Underhill, spent in making
preparations for their journey inland, both Sheppard and Lapsley
experienced their first malarial fevers. Little did Lapsley dream
that he was describing the very place at which he himself in a few
short months, would be laid to rest, a victim of a severe malarial
attack that would result in the dreaded blackwater fever. Below the
mission station on the riverbank was a cluster of corrugated iron
warehouses where the Baptist missions stored the goods brought
in by steamers. "A little further back, in the hollow of the hill,"
wrote Lapsley "are the graves of the men who pioneered this
work—a sacred spot!"

On Sunday, June 15, Lapsley led the English service at Underhill, reading Moody's "Divine Choice of Instruments" as the devotional. Sheppard was in bed again with fever. At dinner Lapsley himself was discovered to have a temperature of 103 degrees and was sent to bed. During the night both men had temperatures of 105 degrees, but were over the fever by morning.[16]

Caravan Journey around Livingstone Falls
June 17, 1890–July 18, 1890

At 3 A.M. on Tuesday, June 17, Lapsley and his caravan began their 230-mile trek around the rapids of the Congo River. Sheppard, still too sick to walk, was carried in a canvas hammock slung onto a sturdy pole, borne on the shoulders of two muscular carriers. Lapsley described their caravan and manner of traveling in his diary:

> We had 25 men in all, and made quite an imposing caravan. Our bedding rolled up and put in big valises, and our bedsteads took three men. Two carried the tent; two took our "pocket-book," which contained 75 dozen red bandanna handkerchiefs and 37 twelve-yard pieces of checked domestic. Four men carried the trunks; one, the table, chairs and guns. One bore on his head the "chop-box"—three feet long, twelve inches wide and eight inches deep, containing corned beef, jam, hard bread and crackers, lard, butter, salt, tea, coffee and sugar, all sealed up in tins. Another carried the "canteen," which was a big bucket, with a nice little kettle, sauce-pan, tea and sugar holders, dishes, two each; plates, cups, large and small spoons, knives and forks, all fitting in under one cover, so that they could not be jostled while on the march.

> There were two canvas hammocks with pillows inside and a shawl spread across the pole—jump in and the men trot off as if they had no load at all.

It was fine to walk as fast as I could for an hour, then call up the hammock men, climb in and rest, while they made even better time than if I were walking. In this way we traveled fast without getting tired. The caravan made a most interesting sight as they moved off, Indian file, up the hill. You could just see a line of black backs showing above the grass, with a big bundle on top of each. One of our men carried a load of 102 pounds, and always got to camp among the first.

Our mode of travel each day was to start before sunrise, after a good breakfast, rest after dinner until 2 o'clock, then march for two hours or more. Before sundown we stopped and camped, always by a stream of water. The *Capita*, or head man of the carriers, sweeps a place clean for the tent, soon it is up, all the cords over the pegs, the water-proof floor in, the beds made and the mosquito nets spread. Meanwhile, the men have made several fires, and a carrier has brought water. The "chop-box" and canteen are opened, the table and chairs untied and set up, an early supper, then bed.

We are very fond of walking, besides, it was inspiring to feel with every step that we were that much further on our way towards the real work we had come to do. We met numerous ivory caravans with loads amounting to at least five tons, and a few caravans with rubber.

We would have had a very different trip six months later on. Then, it would be both disagreeable and dangerous, very hot,—a kind of steaming heat from wet earth and grass—big rains, drenching everything on short notice, and making great torrents of the little stream that crosses the road every half mile. Now it is the dry season, the Congo winter, and everything is favorable for the road.[17]

Halfway between Matadi and the Pool, Lapsley and Sheppard reached the transport center called Lukunga, where the carriers from Matadi returned home and others were hired to carry the loads the rest of the way to the Pool.

Here Lapsley had further opportunity to observe mission work firsthand. He wrote:

> Mr. Hoste, an outstanding missionary of the American Baptist Missionary Union, has a good work here. He is very gentle, and loves the native people with a passion and gives himself entirely to preaching and looking after the boys he has gathered in a boarding school. I believe this concentration and similar plans at Banza-Manteke, have made these the only markedly successful mission stations in the Congo.[18]

At Lukunga, Lapsley himself made his first effort to preach to his carriers in "white man's *Fiote* [trade lingo]." With excitement he wrote: "There was little I could say, still I could tell the story of Jesus and they understood me. We were in touch!"

Riverboat Travel on the Upper Congo
July 31, 1890–December 3, 1890

On July 18, the caravan passed the final cataract and reached the placid twenty-four-mile-long body of water above it, called Stanley Pool, where the Congo River pauses before its precipitous leaps down to the sea. Along its shores at Kinshasa, renamed Leopoldville for the king, could be seen six different French, Dutch, and Belgian settlements, each one the base of a chain of posts extending upriver into the heart of the Congo Free State. Lapsley was immediately impressed with the primary importance of riverboat travel on the Upper Congo waterways:

> The communication between each base and its outposts is maintained by one or more steamboats, made in Europe in small pieces, weighing less than a hundred weight each, transported on the heads of the Congo natives to the Pool, and there rebuilt and launched. This is very wonderful to me, and to make it more so, I know of at least five new steamers on the way up or already being put together.

Here we find people from most of the tribes on the upper
river. In countenance and physique they are superior to the
people we have seen. Their districts are far more populous,
according to what I can hear. It is among these we seek a
field of labor.[19]

The missionaries were comfortably lodged at the American
Baptist Missionary Union compound under the direction of
Dr. Sims. They expressed deep appreciation for the priceless advice
and help freely given them and the way in which "events shaped
so as to lead us plainly thus far, far more than we can realize. Truly
God has been mindful of us."

On July 31, 1890, Lapsley left on the American Baptist steamer,
the *Henry Reed*, for a five-day journey upriver to Bolobo, the
mission station of the famous missionary explorer, Rev. George
Grenfell. Sheppard remained in Leopoldville to begin making
arrangements and to hire boatmen for their own projected
Kwango explorations in native dugout canoes.[20]

For three months Lapsley traveled along the Upper Congo,
visiting not only Bolobo, where Rev. and Mrs. Grenfell lived, but
other mission posts founded by him. He seized every opportunity
to talk with experienced missionaries and observe their methods
and the results of their labor.

He learned much on this fascinating river voyage. He saw for
the first time the amazing variety and abundance of Central
African wildlife. Huge crocodiles basked on the sandbanks;
immense hippo heads rose snorting from the water; elephant,
buffalo, and deer tracks covered the beaches; and myriads of water
birds, cranes, storks, egrets, as well as flocks of ducks and guinea
fowl fed in the tall grasses and reeds along the river's edge.

The young missionary also saw for the first time the raw, brutal
lifestyle of some of the Congolese. While on the *Henry Reed*, he saw
the headless body of a murdered man floating in the river.

At Bwemba, weeping women were heard "mourning beside
the emaciated corpse of a man, his body covered with red
camwood." A little further on, in this same village, they met old
Chief Ebenda, quite drunk, who gleefully pointed to a pile of

seven skulls beside his house. That same afternoon, they heard "rapid, triple-measured drum-beat in the town south of the mission, indicating drinking and dancing." They went to investigate and "saw a woman sentenced by the king for lewdness and idleness. Her grave was half dug, her head decorated by the women, and she waiting the end, when Mr. Billington interceded and had her spared by payment of 100 brass rods.[21]

At a town north of Bolobo he saw a corpse regally dressed, sitting in state in a chair. His head was crowned with a large bunch of rooster feathers and his face painted several different colors. Six weeping women, wearing only fringed belts of grass and green bark, were dancing slowly around him, monotonously chanting the traditional death wail.

During Sunday breakfast at Bolobo, a frantic runner called the Grenfells to the scene of a murder. The body of the dead man had been pierced repeatedly with spears "to find evidence of his being a witch."

In spite of such unnerving sights, George Grenfell always maintained a quiet, steady, confident manner that was very reassuring to Lapsley. The old missionary had long discussions with the young one, covering every sort of mission work policy and explaining every phase of the work of the Baptist Missionary Society. On the basis of his own explorations, he urged Lapsley to go to the Kasai.

On August 7, Lapsley wrote in his diary:

> Much sense of the reality of my work, and of things divine for me! Am copying the maps of the Kwango lent to me by Mr. Grenfell, according to the survey made by him in 1880. Aside from their utility, these maps are very interesting as finished scientific work of the highest order.[22]

The amazing scope of Grenfell's geographical research is attested to by his honorary membership in the Royal Geographical Society of England, awarded for his wonderful, detailed map of the entire Congo Basin. In 1884, he explored the Congo River up to the equator on a small steam vessel. That same year he launched the first mission steamer, *The Peace,* at Stanley Pool. This was the steamer on which he explored the Busira River and discovered the dwarf Batwa tribe. In 1886 he explored the Upper Kasai, the Sankuru, the Luebo and the Lulua Rivers, the very area soon to be occupied by the American Presbyterian Congo Mission. He even made careful records of the Bakuba and Bakete ethnic groups, those with which Lapsley and Sheppard would begin their work.

On November 10, Lapsley visited one of Grenfell's northern-most stations. To his mother he wrote:

> Manyanga is at the head of a stretch of barely navigable water, of which Isangila is at the lower end. Just a little way above here, I believe is the rapid where Frank Pocock, Stanley's last white man on the first trip, was drowned. I can see the white caps and the waves; they dart up like pale silver flames, at this distance. Such another river never was, to be sure! Through this cataract region are scores of villages hiding under the trees, on hill tops, or nestling in the valleys. All of these people are accessible, curious, docile, anxious to work for wages and easily brought under influence.
>
> I am getting impatient to find my own flock, and have a longing, not unnatural, to be face to face with my own life work. Yet the longer God protracts the preparation, the more my gain. I need it! I am very happy! I enjoy more of God's presence now than for sometime past.[23]

The Kwango-Kwilu River Area: A Closed Door
December 11, 1890–February 1, 1891

The apostle Paul and Samuel Lapsley had one thing in common. At a certain stage in their missionary journeying, they both headed in the wrong direction and were very deliberately turned around. When Paul attempted to enter certain provinces of Asia Minor, "the Spirit of Jesus would not allow them to" (Acts 16:7). Instead, the door to Macedonia and all of Europe was thrown open!

When Lapsley determined to explore the Kwango-Kwilu River area with a view to establishing a station there, he and his coworker, Sheppard, were made to realize that this was not the direction in which to go.

In the light of both King Leopold's and George Grenfell's advice that the new outreach be in the direction of the Kasai River area, one wonders why the Kwango-Kwilu region was explored first. Stanley Schaloff, in his *Reform in Leopold's Congo*, suggests that it was simply because of Lapsley's and Sheppard's "determination born of innocence and inexperience" that they took this perilous venture. The result was the most harrowing, dangerous five weeks they had yet faced, but an important time of preparation for their future work.[24]

There were certain happy, lighthearted features of this trip that relieved the tensions. Lapsley's deepening appreciation of Sheppard is evident in many of his letters. To his mother he wrote:

> Sheppard is a most handy fellow and is now a thorough river-man. His temper is bright and even—really a man of unusual graces and strong points of character! The local people think there is nobody like "Mundele Ndom," the "Black White Man," as they call Sheppard. I am happy to think that you pray both for him and for me.

A new member of the caravan also added a spark of fresh enjoyment. At Stanley Falls, a fellow passenger on the *Afrikaan* had given Sheppard the gift of a monkey, to which his new owner promptly gave the name "Tippu-Tip," that of a famous slaver-chief. Lapsley reported that "Sheppard's monkey afforded unbounded amusement to the villagers, chasing and running from them by turns, and finding shelter on Sheppard's shoulder."[25]

The first problem the travelers faced was securing oarsmen to man the two dugout canoes. Sheppard had gone all the way from the Pool back to Lukunga to hire men. When they arrived at Leopoldville and found out where they were going, the men deserted and returned home. The Kwango was alien territory, belonging to their sworn enemies, the Yaka. Sheppard finally persuaded seventeen daring souls from other ethnic groups who were willing to go, although somewhat reluctantly.

River travel was extremely dangerous at that time of year, the height of the rainy season. Sometimes the current was so strong that the boatmen had to "jump into the boiling water, and standing on rocks we couldn't have guessed were there, put the boat through between the stones and past the bad water" by sheer human force.

Lapsley recorded another terrifying experience:

> A big storm came last night, but Sheppard was equal to it. He ran here and there, always in the nick of time and saved the canoes from being swept down to Banana. He swung on the guy rope just as its peg gave way and the tent was getting ready to fly overland to Kintamo![26]

Some of the experiences they had with herds of hippos on this trip were risky, to say the least. Out of food for their boatmen, the missionaries asked them, "In this hostile country, what shall we do?" They were told that if they killed a hippo, local people would be willing to trade the meat for *kwanga*, the staple food made from cassava root. In this way, a contact might be made.

Lapsley wrote:

> So, we found a bay just full of hippos, fifty perhaps. A lively cannonading began. Quick as one let his head come well in sight within a hundred yards, a bullet went that way. You ought to hear them roar, until Sheppard got one right in the center of the forehead and it is finished.
>
> Back to camp and a picked crew detailed to go and watch the hippo rise. They camped all night near where the dead hippo went down. The other hippos made it lively for them. Neither campfire nor brandishing of torches nor shooting could keep them from coming on land, sniffing and snorting within forty feet of the distracted oarsmen. Batula and Kwininga had hysterics and cried like babies.

> At dawn on New Year's Day, we heard a shout, "Come with
> the canoe!" At great risk of turning over, Nkala and his gang
> drew the big pile of meat to shallow water. Then the fun
> began![27]

Time and again, when evening came and a safe place to camp
on shore was being sought, the local people shouted and pointed
guns at them, refusing to let them land. The boatmen explained to
the missionaries that this was because the Congolese thought they
were devils and if they camped near them, they might carry off
some villagers by night.

On the evening of January 16, having consistently been
prevented from landing, they finally were forced to camp in a thick
forest, beside a worn elephant path down to the water. Lapsley's
description of this incident reads:

> A loud noise startled us and I heard the cook exclaim,
> "Nyau!" [elephant]. Sheppard went to see about him and
> presently we heard the crack of his rifle. I hurried through
> the tangle of brush and broken trees to share the hunt. I
> heard Sheppard say in a queer voice, meant for me to hear
> and not the elephant, "Don't come! They are right here!"
>
> Behold! He and Nkala were safe up a tree—an example
> which I promptly followed! Sheppard had put the Martini-
> Henri bullet into the elephant's ear, but when the brute
> seemed unconcerned about it, he did not try another shot
> until he had made sure his retreat. The elephant went away
> for a while but we heard it before day, breaking down trees
> not far from the tent. The woods here look as if a cyclone has
> been throwing trees about.[28]

With increasing frequency Lapsley wrote of bouts of malarial
fever: "Monday: Had fever, only well again Thursday. . . . I have
had many deadly chills from which I seem to rally but slowly. . . .
Found Sheppard hot and put him to bed."

Continually faced with an adamantly belligerent, fearful reception; extreme difficulty in securing food; rumors of trouble with the

state officials, storms, illness; and hungry, reluctant oarsmen who constantly threatened to turn back, the decision was finally made:

> January 21—We conclude to turn back. My men are discouraged, and one is sick and not much time is left on their contracts. They need no persuading to get ready for the down trip![29]

It is significant that, in spite of a heavy heart, Lapsley's diary at this time contains several of the songs his boatmen whistled or sang as they paddled along. His keen appreciation of the native music gave him a measure of happy release from the tensions of the journey.

On their way upriver, the missionaries had stayed for some time at Boleke, a large village at the confluence of the Kasai with the Kwango. There they had found the people friendly and had surveyed for the site of a mission station, in case they did not find a suitable location elsewhere. They had made an agreement with the local chief that on their return, they would make the agreement binding.

On their way back downriver on January 27, Sheppard and Lapsley were hoping for a good reception at Boleke. Instead of welcoming them, the people had nothing to do with them and were quite evidently delighted when they left. The missionaries realized it was no use to wait any longer. Lapsley wrote: "We dropped sadly down stream. Something awful seems to have happened between the natives and the State!"[30]

At Kwamouth, on January 30, they learned from the Catholic brothers over a cup of coffee that there had been serious trouble between the Belgian military "Van Kerckhoven Expedition" and the people. The small "army of State troopers sent to overawe and pacify the country" had burned Chumbiri and the village across the river from Mushie, which Lapsley and Sheppard and their boatmen had seen in smoking ruins as they had passed. The whole countryside was now up in arms! Resentment and fear engendered by the actions of the expedition were further heightened by the captain of a steamer who had taken on a full load of firewood

and then left without paying for it! Hearing all this the missionaries realized that they could not have ventured into the Kwango
area at a worse time. Everything had been against them![31]

On February 1, the two canoes finally reached Leopoldville.
Very definitely the door to the Kwango-Kwilu area had been
closed. It was to the region that Lapsley called, in a letter to his
mother, "the untouched Kasai," that they would now go.

To Luebo on the Steamer *Florida*
March 14, 1891–April 18, 1891

Excerpts from a letter written by Lapsley to his father from
Leopoldville reveal the plans and preparations being made for the
upriver journey:

> Leopoldville, Congo Independent State,
> March 10, 1891
>
> Dear Papa,
> Well, I know much more about business today than I did
> twelve months back, when we took the London and
> Northwestern from Liverpool to London. "Hitherto hath the
> Lord helped us," I am very sure, and it gives me good hope
> that He means for us to do good out here. I am awaiting
> only the steamer which shall take us up the great river,
> which we have come to regard quite as our home. Though
> we go like Abraham, "Not knowing whither we go," we are
> possessed with a desire for a full occupation of the whole
> Kasai valley, and trust Him to show us the strategic point to
> begin the attack.
>
> It seems to have been ordered by Providence that we should
> come at the very instant the Kasai is being opened. The
> *Societe Anonyme Belge* has completed and equipped their line
> of stations up the Congo to the Falls, and intends this year,
> within six months, to open four new stations on the Kasai,
> besides the one they have at Luebo. To their two 500-load
> steamers, they are adding two 1,000-load steamers and two

more small ones. One of the big boats is coming up now; the rest are almost finished at Kinshasa today.[32]

Major Parminter, who is director of the *Societe Anonyme Belge* in this country, amenable to the administration in Brussels, will not promise to carry any of my loads to the exclusion of his own loads. But he showed me that since rubber is the staple of the Kasai trade, and is cheaper to the bulk than cloth, there will, of necessity, be less cargo on up-trips than down. So, I need not doubt the feasibility of carrying on our limited transport through the S.A.B.; there is always passenger room, and down-trips are half rates. I think we shall suffer from delays, etc., until we do our own transport with a Presbyterian Mission steamer.[33]

While the missionaries were patiently waiting for the *Stanley* to arrive from upriver, Sheppard suddenly discovered on Friday, March 14, that the *Florida* was already tied up at the Kinshasa riverbank getting loaded for a trip up the Congo and Kasai to Luebo. It was to leave at 6 A.M. the following Tuesday. They had so little time in which to complete arrangements! Lapsley recorded in his diary:

I went to Kinshasa, to the *Societe Anonyme Belge* station, where the *Florida* lay. Mr. Clotens, the manager, sent for the Captain of the *Florida*, and we proposed that they would take for us forty loads, with our canoe tied alongside.

"Impossible!" said the Captain to Mr. Clotens. "We would never get up the Kasai with the poor pressure our lame boiler can make, and you won't let me stop to make adequate repairs!"

So, they had it up and down! Finally, Mr. Clotens agreed to take Sheppard and me, eight carriers and twenty loads, each load being seventy pounds.

"Small allowance!" said I, when I went back to talk it over with Sheppard.

"And no canoe," said Sheppard, "but this is our only chance before August, unless we canoe it again."

So, we concluded that we would make a grave mistake in not accepting.[34]

Their next hurdle was getting licenses from the state to employ the carriers that they were taking with them. Licenses were granted only at the capital, Boma. Dr. Sims came to their rescue by persuading "the obliging young acting Commissioner, Caiton," to employ them himself and give them to the missionaries, bound by contract for one year.

Sheppard canoed their loads to the *Florida*, getting back to the Baptist Missionary Society guest house by 7 P.M. At 9 P.M., they began the tramp along the shore "through the dew and uncertain

The *Florida*, *steamer on which Lapsley and Sheppard journeyed up the Kasai and Lulua Rivers to Luebo. Courtesy—Musée Royale de l'Afrique Centrale, Tervuren, Belgique.*

light of the setting moon, six or eight miles to the steamer."
Lapsley carried Mr. Clotens's receipt for a check for sixty British
sterling pounds for their passage to Luebo, men and loads
included. They made "the most momentous departure since that
from New York on Wednesday February 26, last year!" They had
determined that the future dominant Kasai tribes were the allied
Bakuba, Bashilange, and Baluba, living in and near the ellipse
formed by the Kasai, Sankuru, Lubi, and Zambezi Rivers. Now
Lapsley and Sheppard were certain that they were headed in the
right direction!

As the paddle wheeler started churning and the *Florida* moved
away from the bank, Lapsley found himself singing a hymn he had
learned while he was in England:

> Wherever He may guide me, no want shall turn me back;
> My Shepherd is beside me and nothing can I lack.
> His wisdom ever waketh, His eyes are never dim;
> He knows the way He taketh, and I will walk with Him.

The seven-by-nine-foot dining room was assigned the two
missionaries as their sleeping quarters. They stretched their
bedrolls along the benches on either side of a battered mahogany
table. This was luxury compared to camping on a storm-swept
sandbank! Lapsley described the captain as having an "uncom-
monly simple and pleasing politeness, desiring only that we be
comfortable and satisfied."[35]

Once again their path crossed that of the Van Kerckhoven
Expedition. Sheppard went ashore in a canoe at Lisa, the first state
post upriver from Stanley Pool, and found it completely deserted.
As the journey progressed, through the very area Lapsley and
Sheppard had so recently visited, the captain of the *Florida* had the
same difficulty in securing food for his crew that the missionaries
had had for their oarsmen. At every village, the people would
simply melt into the forest at the sight of a white man. No one
dared to venture out to trade, not even for things that they needed
and wanted. Only Sheppard was the passenger least feared, with
whom a few hardy souls would sometimes dare to dicker!

The giant river system of the Congo straddles the equator, causing the rainy and dry seasons to alternate on either side of it. In March, when this river journey took place, the waters of the Upper Congo were low, while those of the Kasai, fed by the Kwango-Kwilu and Sankuru, were at flood stage. The result at Kwamouth, where the two meet, is a deadly maelstrom which has swallowed up many a river steamer. This is the very spot where the first mission paddle wheeler, named for Lapsley, would capsize on November 16, 1903, with great loss of life.

The passage of the *Florida* through this treacherous vortex is graphically described in Lapsley's diary:

> March 20—Getting along very slowly, reaching Kwamouth after dinner instead of midmorning. We have only a small amount of wood, and can't venture into a strong river like the Kasai, which is bad for wood, too. So, we must stop and [load] wood at the mouth. As we turned that way we saw a black cloud behind the hilly bank. Lightnings licked out red tongues, like a mad snake, up and down the black sheet, but we got around the rocky point. The winds and current were then too strong for us, keeping us ten minutes in one spot, waiting. The waves began to pitch the boat from side to side and up and down, and I fully expected her to go down. But after a fearful passage we were dashed against the sandy beach, a little way above a long line of rocks, and got back to our wooding place after all, shortly before dark.

> Just then, we saw a steamer coming out of the Kasai and stopping a mile above us. I ran over and found that the steamer was the *Stanley* and Captain Matson and the little Dutchman, the engineer, were very cordial and merry to have gotten out of the Kwango without bullet holes in them. They were attacked furiously and persistently for days on the way. The natives were well-armed and their bullets went through thick plank, and they each had narrow escapes from flying bullets. . . .

> With five hours' steaming, we have made only a half-hour's progress, constantly struggling with a desperate mill-tail

affair that shoots down between a wall of boulders and a reef of sand and big black angular rocks. Just think of the whole Kasai pressed into a current about 150 yards across!

Sheppard was at the wheel and just edging through the last of the bad part—pop! and a noise of a dragging chain. The rudder chain had broken and there were the rocks awaiting us. I ran for a piece of wire I knew about; Sheppard ran back and took charge of the rod connecting and controlling the rudders themselves, and put her into the sandbank ten yards below the rocks.

"And the fire-bars are no good," came from the engineer, Mr. Sirex.

"What's to be done?" asks the captain.

"We'll never make it, let's go back to Kinshasa." But the captain would not agree to go back.

These two well-disposed men can't understand each other, the least cause of this being that Mr. Sirex, the engineer, a Dane, speaks no French, but tolerably fair English, but the captain speaks only French! So, as interpreter, I had a chance to mediate between them, with the key to the position in my hands. No matter what was said, nothing offensive got from one to the other.[36]

The captain was now desperately in need of food for his men. Of the ship's crew, Lapsley said, "Such a pitiable lot of fellows! Not a square meal for a week almost and hardly a crumb for two days and plenty of hard work all the while!" In spite of their desperate need, the captain refused to stop at Mushie, where his predecessor as captain had been killed. Even at the village at the mouth of the Kwango, where Sheppard and Lapsley had applied for their first mission station, he was too afraid of the people there to stop. Finally, farther upriver, they came to some villages where the captain tied bandanna handkerchiefs to a long pole and waved them from the deck as an invitation to the residents to come out in their canoes and trade. To the delight of the crew, there was a quick response and there followed brisk trading in chickens, eggs, cassava, and dried hippo meat.

Lapsley himself was not sick during this river journey, but Sheppard was quite ill, as was the only other passenger, a state official named Simar, bound for Luluabourg with twenty soldiers. Lapsley took some of the canned food for Luebo out of the cases and prepared it for his patients, who were quite unable to "keep down" the usual shipboard fare. He also gave his own bed to Simar and went to sleep out on the deck. The treatment given them was: "Ipecac to begin with, then Dover's powders, quinine and a calomel-jalap tablet every few hours and they produced visible results, under God's favor, and a fresh constitution!"[37]

On March 30, a violent storm overtook them.

> A little above and away from a line of rocks, the wind and waves became too much for the big boat and slow engine, and drove us broadside right into the bushes. There was a fearful crash of breaking branches, rushing water and smashing woodwork. We waited for a calm, with only a battered cabin to grieve for, the captain's bridge having gone into a big tree!

Another threatening episode occurred on April 15. Lapsley recorded:

> We made a good, long day's progress, but late in the afternoon came very near being wrecked in a very simple piece of water. There is a strong point where two down currents meet from above and rush around it with tremendous force. This forms great swirls in the line of the current below, and a strong back current on either side of the united current below the point. We came up near the bank and steered across the strong water. When the bow got into the down current, the stern was still in the up current and of course the steamer got a sharp turn-around. This performance was repeated several times; the boat was wheeled around like a floating stick and went full speed toward the bank. By a

special Providence the steamer was turned in time, so that, though we were much frightened, no damage resulted.[38]

April 16—We were delayed by the hanging of the anchor. Sheppard joined the divers, who ascertained that it was caught fast in a limb fifteen feet down. He went down the chain, hand under hand. Afterwards he and Macaulay hauled it out with a windlass, the steamer pulling a little also. At noon we stopped again for wood, and lost about two hours by a repetition of the morning's frolic with the anchor.[39]

As the *Florida* neared Luebo, having turned into the Lulua River, tributary to the Kasai, the missionaries noted a marked difference in the terrain. Now there were rolling grassland savannas, with thick forests along the rivers and nestled in the pockets between the hills. The crowds that gathered around them at wood stops were bigger than before and the people friendly. Lapsley's description of the residents in his diary reads:

Nice looking people. Cleanly, head shaved, except a chignon at the apex, and this topped by a natty little cap, fastened on with ivory or fancy brass hairpins, lady fashion. Picturesque effect, erect, graceful, easy carriage, clean, dark body, gathered yellow cloth skirt hanging from the waist.[40]

On April 18, 1891, the *Florida* rounded the last bend in the river and the government post on the bank came into sight. Lapsley describes what happened as they landed:

At noon we rounded Luebo point. All of us are on the bridge, the station is astir. Soldiers and workmen and a crowd of others are rushing about. Our boatmen have gotten the drum, which Mr. Simar used as a seat at the table, and are dancing to its accompaniment now. Our glad hosts prospective are shouting welcome from the bank to those they know, and station workers are pointing out to each other, faces and objects they recognize on board. Now we are ashore, meeting the two agents for the company and the agent for the State, and the Commissaire du District du Kasai, who may be able to help us greatly in our plans, by giving at once his sanction to our application for land.

We are advised to locate across on the north side of the Lulua, halfway between the Luebo government post and the Bakete town of Bena Kasenga, the latter being about twenty minutes walk uphill from the river crossing. I am pretty sure of getting this place. You may safely think of me as here, busy and happy.[41]

Founding of American Presbyterian Congo Mission April 19, 1891–November 19, 1891

As Lapsley watched the *Florida* leave for the return trip to Kinshasa and the Pool, he felt "some sadness, some solitude, but much joy and satisfaction." Captain Galhier assured him that in nine months the riverboat would make a return trip to Luebo.

A walk down the steep hill and a canoe ride across the Lulua River took the new missionary to the Belgian post for his first visit as a Luebo resident. On the way, Lapsley stepped over the first big African snake he had seen and made his first purchase, some palm oil, to make a lamp—"simply a plaited rag lying in a cup of oil, one end out."

Sheppard, the born trader, quickly acquired a large, wooden mortar for pounding the starchy manioc roots into flour and "a very nice portable native house, ten feet, eight inches square on the inside and nine feet, six inches high at the roof peak. He also exchanged five little bells for 200 cowry shells," the most desired medium of trade in that region.[42]

During the night Lapsley heard a great commotion:

Sheppard was moving about very rapidly, and even dancing, and addressing the people in impassioned tones. On inquiry, I learned that a column of driver ants had entered his house and taken possession. They even came under the blankets and covered him; hence, his animation. They happened to be marching by and smelt the palm oil inside.

> We made various reconnaissances with torches and candles, found many columns pouring across the open space near his house, and many large bodies deployed as skirmishers. One line had reached my tent door just as I got up. A fire stopped them. I looked around and met another body of them making for the back of the tent, where there was a greasy spot, black with them. . . . Sheppard slept in the moonlight after that![43]

Lapsley acquired his own dwelling the next day, one a bit superior to Sheppard's. The latter's house had only a long window by which to enter, while Lapsley's had both a door and a window! Bakete houses are made of thick palm ribs lashed together with forest vines, each wall a section in itself that can be fitted together with the end of another section. Such "collapsible" houses permit entire villages to be picked up and moved overnight to a new site, at the chief's command. They are surprisingly sturdy and excellent protection from sun and rain.

The two missionaries felt that they really were home when they finished "landscaping," planting a row of pineapples and plantain trees in front of each house! Lapsley also acquired his first musical instrument for which he paid two-cents worth of brass wire. It was a native mandolin made of a gourd for resonance, with a staff and three strings.[44]

Another night brought the new experience of an invasion of termites: "White ants infest the damp earth. They crawled up the bedpost and riddled a hole in my mattress before morning, big as my hand."

Lapsley and Sheppard were impressed with how industrious the people were:

> Busy folks! Very few without something to do! The principle business outside of manioc bread-making, the main occupation of the women, is the making of a native cloth called *madiba*.

I watched the manufacture of it in all its stages: boys strip-
ping off the outside leaf of the palm leaf blade, leaving the
delicate green ribbons within, then tying them into hanks,
like yarn. Men were separating these strips and threading
them through a loom with the warp. Then came the clack of
the simple, but complete weaving machine! The women
pound a few choice pieces in a mortar till they are soft and
satiny. These are dyed, sewn together and, worn on special
occasions.

It is an important fact that these people like to work and
know how to *hire out*. Some Congo tribes won't do it for love
nor money![45]

I like the native folks very much. They are not stuck up,
though they are ready to stand up for themselves, and they
like to keep on good terms. They are very funny and lively,
and make good company. They keep pretty clean, especially
those that live by the water-side, who have skins like velvet,
soft and smooth. They all believe in sweeping their yards and
houses in the town (and no African but lives in town). If any
fellow is lazy about it, they call a town meeting, and make
him pay the price of five chickens or a goat, and the rest have
a feast at his expense, which makes them all careful.[46]

To his brother James, Lapsley gave more details of the founding
of the new mission station. He himself had made a little veranda
addition to the front of his ten-foot-square house, giving it a "hip-
roof, like those in the front and rear of our old Vine Hill house." A
garden plot had been prepared, scrub and tall grass cleared away,
and milk goats and a small flock of chickens acquired.

Foremost on Lapsley's mind, however, was learning the native
language:

I have picked up some ten or dozen words of Kikete, but not
enough yet to do any good. I have learned the words for
"chicken" "plenty," "little," "good" and "no" or "not." The
little Kikongo I picked up in lower Congo helps greatly.
Sheppard has a little Kikongo and less Kikete, but he is

powerful on signs! I hope immediately to begin cramming
my note-book and head with words and idioms I can pick
up constantly, even from the children, who love to come and
pull up grass for a few cowries, and from people I meet
every hour. Before long, I hope to begin to give them ideas
of our Savior's life and death, and of His interest in their
souls. Perhaps in six months I can stand up and speak before
a formal concourse of people.

With excitement he wrote a few days later: "Today I got both
nouns and verbs from a party trading and chattering in my house.
I used the words as soon as I caught them in what I guessed was
their meaning and I was understood at once!"[47]

From the very beginning of their arrival in the Congo,
Sheppard and Lapsley had held daily services with their native
helpers. Lapsley wrote to his brother Bob:

Recently I asked Sheppard to take charge of the daily meetings and gave him full swing. I was surprised to come in one
day and find that he had had them all pray aloud. Two of
our new workers have developed some gifts of expressing
their desires, showing their interest in the services and an
improved demeanor in all other matters. I intend to tran-
scribe for you one of Ngosole's prayers. They are edifying,
and often strikingly fresh and appropriate![48]

On May 6, 1891, Lapsley and Sheppard made a map of the
mission station site and wrote a formal application to occupy it.
They both went over to see the commissaire and present it to him.
He promised to send the application, with his approval, to the
governor general of the Congo Free State in Boma for final ratifi-
cation of the American Presbyterian Congo Mission.[49]

The commissaire and his aide came by the new station for a
visit. He seemed quite pleased with the progress already made. He
had the chief gather the village people together and told them that
they must sell to the missionaries at fair prices "and after a while,
when they have a good house for a school, you must send your
children to learn to read and write and work at useful trades." As

he left, he told the missionaries, "If I can help you in any way, write me at Luluabourg."[50]

The sure sign that Lapsley and Sheppard had been accepted and had made a real impression on the people was the fact that they had been given their own native names. Sheppard was called Ngela, or "The Hunter" and Lapsley's name was *Mutomba Njila*, the "The Pathfinder," meaning "The Forerunner." Zairiens have a rare gift of perceiving character and giving a name particularly suited to a personality. Both Lapsley and Sheppard now had names indicative of the work they would do.[51]

Life was seldom monotonous for the missionaries. There were always lighthearted or exciting events that relieved the burden they carried for their work.

Sheppard gave a delightful description of an amusing experience Lapsley had when he was still a curiosity to those around him, who had rarely seen a "white man":

> The Bakete, after having seen Mr. Lapsley's face and hands and making close examination of both, were anxious to see his feet. They begged and pleaded with him—men, women and children—to pull off his shoes and socks (his socks they called "bags") that they might get one peep, at least. To satisfy the crowd Mr. Lapsley exhibited his small, clean, white feet. The eyes of the people opened wide. They laughed, talked and pulled at each other, so pleased! Then, they got on their knees and began to handle them. Mr. Lapsley was ticklish under the bottoms of his feet and this caused him to join in with the admirers in a hearty laugh.[52]

Sheppard also recorded the following incidents:

> One morning as Mr. Lapsley's door blew open a native saw a strange sight. It was Mr. Lapsley on his knees by his couch with his face in his Bible praying. The native was anxious to know of me what it all meant, and so I had the pleasure of explaining to him that Mr. Lapsley, their friend, was talking to the Great King above, about them. The native was so pleased he ran back to the town and told it to the people. . . .

Another day as Mr. Lapsley's face was shining with divine
brightness, and as he was putting his whole soul into his
sermon on God's love, to a large crowd of natives, a woman
who was the leader of the town dances was so deeply
touched that she arose, stretched forth her long arms and
said distinctly and earnestly, "Why, Mr. Lapsley, if we had
known God loved us we would have been singing to Him."
Mr. Lapsley was so overcome that he could say but little
more. The Holy Spirit had made a deep impression on
Malemba's heart, and she was almost yielding.[53]

From June 6 to August 15, Sheppard was away on an
exploratory trip with a Luebo rubber and ivory trader named
Stache. While he was gone, Lapsley continued to develop many
different aspects of the work which marked him to be a true,
pioneer trailbreaker in founding a new mission. In his letters he
described his way of teaching the writing of the alphabet:

I instruct on the anatomical construction of B-a-ba. I use
charcoal on one of my new planks as a board, and impress
the shape of the new characters on their minds by copying
them with sharp sticks on the dirt floor of the house. "This
is the name of a boy you know well [Baba], see how much
better is this way of indicating him than trying to draw a
picture of him." They began to take an interest in this
concrete style of teaching.[54]

Lapsley, the music lover, continued to dream of the day when
"the great hymns of the church would be sung at Luebo. Just wait
awhile until we sing the gospel in the dialect of the Upper Kasai," he
wrote. Meanwhile, he sang the Kikongo hymns he had learned in the
Lower Congo. The people loved to hear him sing and often gathered
to ask him to sing for them. He also kept noting the "responsive
solos and unison choruses of the fine, strong voices" heard on every
occasion as boatmen paddled canoes, women hoed gardens, or
villagers danced in the moonlight. These were a singing people![55]
He conducted a daily worship service in which he told simple
Bible stories, using Kikongo as well as his rapidly increasing

vocabulary of Kikete words. Always his ears were alert to every word he heard, to hear and understand its use and meaning, which he recorded.

Lapsley also walked in the steps of the Great Physician, helping both black and white with what drugs he had. On July 13, a man came to ask him to go and see Mr. Engeringh, the trader living at the state post across the river. Lapsley wrote:

> I found he has black-water fever (hematuria.) Spent most of the day with him, until with the abatement of the fever, the flow of blood ceased. Quinine, etc., did the work. You will be surprised to know that I have become something of a doctor. How, I don't know, unless by having first to take a good deal of medicine from others, and then learning to dose myself and Sheppard.[56]

His medical ministry to his native friends also had good results. He began to carry his medicine case to the village when he visited and soon had "many cases a day, and they all got well! Three or four were bad ones!" The Bakete chief, Kwete, was one of his patients. Before long, Lapsley's neighbors were singing a song in his honor: "Mutomba Njila gives us medicine! He makes us see life!"[57]

Lapsley was urged by some to ask for a goat in payment for treating a serious illness. They were amazed that he asked nothing for his services. Sheppard commented:

> Mr. Lapsley never charged for medical attention, but many showed appreciation of his kindness by giving him little presents of peanuts, pineapples, bananas or sugar cane. I never saw him more pleased than when a little, laughing girl came stepping up to him and handed him a small string of sun perch. Mr. Lapsley had been her doctor when she was down with fever.[58]

When a Bena Kasenga chief presented Lapsley with the gift of his ten-year-old son, it became evident that now the mission work was to take a new direction. A thirty-foot-long dormitory was constructed for housing both the chief's son and the large group of

other boys and young men who had come to live near the missionaries and learn from them.

Sheppard returned from his trip to find Lapsley quite ill again
with fever. The two discussed their original choice of a location site
in the forest and decided to move to another, farther up on the hill,
"more pleasant, cool and healthful."

On August 28, they bought a third house to use for storage and
had it and their own two "residences" moved to the new site. A
group of Bakete men moved the houses, a side and a roof at a time,
"much as Samson moved the gates of Gaza, only half a dozen men,
instead of one! Queer to see the whole roof trotting along on a
dozen brown legs that show below it"—a cross between a turtle
and a millipede![59]

Part of the new plot they chose had recently been cleared and
used as a manioc field, so it took little work to prepare it for habi-
tation. It was on the hillside, surrounded by fields, a gentle, lightly
wooded slope extending before them all the way down to the
Lulua River. Lapsley envisioned that before long he would see on
that slope "good pastures for cattle!" He noted with evident pleasure, that those who came to live with them in the mission village
enjoyed the new location, and that they danced often at night to
the rhythmic beat of the big drum that he had recently bought for
them.

On October 25, he preached his first sermon in Kikete. A
Christian soldier from Zanzibar, based at the state military post
across the river, let him use his Kiswahili Testament. Owing to the
common origin and similarity of all Bantu languages, Lapsley
found it quite helpful in preparing for his first real sermon in the
local language. At last, he was preaching to his people in their own
language![60]

Journey to Luluabourg (Malange)
November 20, 1891–December 25, 1891

Lapsley had a dual purpose in making the trip on foot to
Luluabourg, the most important state administrative and military

posts in the Kasai River area. Not only did he want to "scout out" the various tribal lands and get to know the people, he also wanted to secure workmen for clearing the property and constructing durable buildings at Luebo. Now that the official petition by the missionaries for a station site concession and civil status for the American Presbyterian Congo Mission had been sent to the governor general of the Congo Free State at Boma, it was important to make definite plans for the future.[61]

Preparations for the journey included mending his travel bag, and counting out thirty-five dozen bandannas, two long pieces of brass wire and four hundred brass rods, thirteen inches long, to use as trade items on the road. A box of provisions and "a covered basket with some changes of raiment" were Lapsley's only personal effects. The caravan crossed the Lulua in the evening and spent the night at Mr. Engeringh's trading post, in order to be off before dawn on the long overland trek southeastward. There were nineteen people in the caravan including Vwila, Lapsley's helper from Lower Congo; Shamba (the lad given to the missionary by his father, the Bakete chief); nine carriers; and seven women. The latter were originally from Malange, abandoned at Luebo by Zanzibari soldiers who, when their contract service ended, left for home on a river steamer. The women had been waiting for months to join any caravan bound for Malange, so that they might travel without danger of being caught and sold into slavery. They proved to be a welcome addition to the party for, being familiar with the path, they led the way, brushing the heavy dew off the tall grasses, finding food, going for water, and cooking dinner for all the caravan members.

Every day the group from Luebo marched for several hours before the heat of the day. Lapsley reported on November 27:

> Today we marched steadily for five hours, threading our way through a great forest. I hardly stopped walking once; was most careful not to sit down and rest, as I find that I hold out better that way. The young caravan members sang snatches of songs, joked and repeated funny things said the day before, trotting along briskly under their light loads.

They covered from ten to thirty miles each day, according to the condition of the foot trail or the time spent visiting with the chiefs of the villages through which they passed.[62]

Lapsley noted the variety of receptions given them in village after village. At one, the "Baluba of the town seem a little surprised, not at seeing just another white man, but such a *tame* one, with well-behaved caravan men!" At Kakomba, they arrived at midmorning "to find it deserted and partly burned, for fear of the State soldiers." At still another, "The people swarmed around me, seemingly greatly pleased at being allowed to look as much as they liked at the new kind of white man." When they commented on how strange it was to have a *gentle* white man in their midst, Lapsley explained that his King, whom they called "Nzambi" (God), loves black men as well as white, so his missionary ambassador "couldn't be bad to them, even if he wanted to!"

One of the highlights of the trek to Luluabourg was the quiet Sunday spent at one village where the young missionary "had the pleasure of explaining the story of the Gospel to the two chiefs and about a hundred of their people." Lapsley found the people most open and receptive, eager to hear and ask questions.[63]

Another highlight occurred when the caravan came to the deserted town of Tshinyama, where the English Presbyterian missionary Dr. Summers had died on his way back to Great Britain:

> It makes me sad to think of him, that so brave and good a man should have been taken away with his work just begun, not able to go on without him! The people loved him very much, and talk about him as if he died only yesterday!

Little did Lapsley dream that these very same words would, in a few short weeks, be applied to him and his own brief life's work of launching the American Presbyterian Congo Mission!

At Kakamba he was offered an unusual treat, to refresh himself on his journey: "I was given quantities of young bees, roasted with a little oil, and what is more, I *ate* quantities of them and found them very nice!"

As Lapsley's caravan neared Luluabourg, they continued to pass through deserted, burned villages—signs of the recent disturbances between the local people and Congo Free State soldiers. In a small brook at the foot of the high hill on which the state post was located, the party paused to splash water on sweat-streaked faces and put on their best apparel. Then, up the wide avenue, lined with trees, they made their way. A Belgian army lieutenant welcomed Lapsley, took him to the official headquarters and introduced him to a young Belgian officer who had just been appointed commissaire of the Kasai District. Comfortable quarters were courteously provided for the missionary during his visit.

On Friday, December 10, he wrote: "I stopped at the State post for several days, looking around, asking people questions, and looking for workmen, for slaves to ransom and for a bull and cow to buy. Not much luck at first!"[64]

Lapsley decided that his best chance of finding what he was looking for was to visit the large Zappo Zappo village adjoining the administrative post. He had learned that two of his good friends from Luebo, Jose, the interpreter, and Seeku, were now living there. As he approached the tall cone-shaped house with a flag floating from the top, the residence of King Zappo Zappo, whom should he meet but young Prince Zappo himself!

It was a providential encounter that Lapsley described in the following manner:

> Zappo is a very handsome young fellow about twenty-three years old. He wore a cloak from the waist to the knees, and another thrown over his shoulders, and a folded handkerchief, tied about his head in a rakish style.
>
> "Is that cloth you have in that bundle? Let's see it." And he led the way back to Seeku, who acted as interpreter, bringing us to an agreement.
>
> Zappo offered some slaves for the heavy blue cloth I showed him, and suggested that I make him a present and arrange it as a matter of friendship rather than of business. I agreed and gave him eighteen yards of the blue cloth, and

> some twenty yards of brass wire, not cut up into rods, seeing he was a king.
>
> Next day I went over to see him, about half an hour's walk. He received me . . . and had his present brought—a good looking boy of nineteen, a girl about sixteen, and a boy of eleven. These young folks were not sorry about the change in ownership, only asking if they were to be sold again.
>
> I said, "No, you are my children now," and I gave them cloth and plenty of food to eat. So, they are immensely pleased![65]

Another fortunate coincidence was that, as Lapsley's caravan left Luluabourg and headed back toward Luebo, the guide lost his way and they reached an out-of-the-way village that they never would have visited. As a result of the unexpected encounter with the people there, Lapsley engaged eleven workmen and wives of five of them. The friendly man who had welcomed him and been his host also agreed to go with the missionary to Luebo and settle there with his family if he found that he liked it.

At a stopover at the post of Saturnino, a friend of Lapsley's added a gift of four pigs to the procession. Now there were "seventeen men, five women, one baby, four pigs and two dozen chickens."[66]

The trip back to Luebo was made more slowly, without hurrying the little folks and livestock, a miscellaneous caravan that, Lapsley remarked, "must have resembled that of the patriarch, Jacob." He reached Luebo in six days, limping the last thirty miles, and dragged into Mr. Engeringh's "down the avenue between the rows of tall banana trees, through the silent post and up to the big front door, where his friends were sitting on the cool veranda in the twilight."[67]

The next morning canoes ferried the whole assemblage across the Lulua River to the mission side. Sheppard states in his writings that in addition to Lapsley's own party, many along his route were so attracted to the loving, gentle-spirited missionary that they later followed his caravan. In many cases, "men with their wives and children, goats, sheep and all their belongings followed him to Luebo." This was the beginning of the large native village that grew up around Luebo mission station, estimated in later years to be some ten thousand in population.

During the ten months that had elapsed since the *Florida* first brought the two missionaries to Luebo, the work that they had come to do was off to a vigorous, wisely directed beginning. God had really blessed the dedicated efforts of both men.

The Final Journey
January 8, 1892–March 26, 1892

Lapsley returned from his Luluabourg journey utterly exhausted. Sheppard, in his book *Presbyterian Pioneers in Congo*, gives a touching description of what happened:

> How happy we were when a runner announced Mr. Lapsley's arrival. With the big ivory horn blowing and the drums beating, we ran down the banana walk to greet and welcome him home. He was tired, worn and weary, and walked with a limp. He had been scorched by the sun, beaten by the rains, and torn by the thorns; his coat was in tatters, and his last pair of shoes worn into holes; but through all of this he had that heaven-born smile as he said, "Sheppard, how are you? I am glad to see you." Soon we had him seated in front of his cabin in a camp chair and a pan of cool fresh water for his tanned face and tired feet.
>
> Our cook killed a goat and a feast of the very best we had followed. I could bear the burning sand with bare feet easier and safer than Mr. Lapsley could, so the last pair of shoes of the camp, though two sizes too large, were brought forth and put on his feet. But I could not refrain from withdrawing to the bushes nearby and there in the quiet I thought of the beautiful Southern home on the hillside in Anniston, Alabama, of the clothing, food and comfort in that home, of the dear hearts of that home who so loved Mr. Lapsley, and I broke down in spirit and wept.
>
> Mr. Lapsley told me the evening of his arrival that every bone in his body ached, and that he felt as though he had

been beaten with rods. A fever soon followed. I nursed him carefully and tenderly through it and he was much improved in color from the purges and quinine.[68]

On January 1, 1892, the *Florida* brought a letter from the governor general of the Congo Free State at Boma, calling Lapsley to the capital to meet with authorities on serious matters relating to the request for a concession and civil status for the American Presbyterian Congo Mission.

This important official business, together with Lapsley's poor health, depleted strength, and need of a change, made it very clear that he should return to the Lower Congo on the *Florida* as it made the return trip downriver.

It was with sad hearts that the first little nucleus of Christian believers in the Kasai watched their beloved friend leave. They knew, however, that he was planning to return as soon as he had finished the business he had with the state. His companion, Sheppard, would be with them, busily carrying on in his absence. In fact, Lapsley heartily endorsed Sheppard's plans to visit, while he was gone, the great Bakuba kingdom, forbidden to the white man. Both men hoped that Sheppard's meeting with the great sovereign Lukengu might open the door to mission work with the Bakuba.[69]

The tired missionary thoroughly enjoyed the downriver trip on the *Florida*. A letter to his father is full of fascinating facts and insights into his plans for the future. On January 8, 1892, Lapsley wrote:

> Today finds me well on the way, and on a very pleasant way. The prospect of meeting old friends and conferring with old advisers, with more intelligent inquiries to make of their experience than when I saw them last; of receiving the new contingent to our mission, with whom we shall be more closely allied than if we were kin almost, if God will; of making up at the Pool the first full, satisfactory equipment for our business that we have known—all this is enough to make me feel light and hopeful.
>
> We are a very congenial party, too, as far as that is possible, outside of the household of faith. Mr. Engeringh, always sturdy, plain, genial, wide awake, and so very kind; Engineer

Van Kouteren, a level-headed Fleming, with a twinkle in his eye; Captain Galhier, well-disposed as ever, and very pleasant, now that things go well; plenty of food aboard, too.

After breakfast, I go up on the bridge, get medicines out of the captain's cupboard, and come down to my seat on a box among the Lagos boat hands forward. They hang their sore legs overboard for the rushing water to wash them for treatment, and come up and present them in turn for medicine. There were nearly twenty sores this morning, some twice the size of a silver dollar. I find a solid satisfaction in easing somewhat their pains—something accomplished!

I have five Lower Congo men on their way to home and pay. Some, perhaps all, will go back to Luebo with me "when they have seen their mothers," as they always say. Then we shall have a nucleus of trusty fellows who will do anything or go anywhere, for I picked them up fresh, and we have trained them.

Mpiata is my majordomo, permanently, I hope; his contract binds him until I go to Mputu (white man's land.) He can speak very fair and very funny English, wash, cook, boss workmen, and is a gilt-edge riverman. Little Mrs. Vwila, his wife, is also aboard, going to see the Congo land, and report back to the Kasai fold.

Shamba Mwana is also taking his first downriver travel, eyes wide open, but not surprised at anything, not he! Nor afraid of anything or anybody. His mother's people raised a terrible row about his father's letting him go to Malange with me in November, and made his life extremely bitter when he got back.

Monday, what was my thankful surprise when Shamba and Musangu came together to the mission and sat down on the veranda. A pause. "Shamba Mwana wants to go with you to the country downriver." "Good!" I say. "I am his father, and Musangu is his mother, and we agree, only we count on your bringing us back a nice gift of cloth and beads."

So the ice is broken at Bena Kasenga! The most popular boy in
Kasenga, known, too, all over the Bakete country, child of two
"royal" houses, has gone to "Mputu" with the missionary.

I wanted to give you an idea of the Kasai, seen as a whole. I
should have given each day's story as it happened, but Mr.
Engeringh and I took a fancy to learn to navigate the
steamer and get something of a pilot's knowledge of its
route among the sandbars. This plan worked nicely for
awhile, but the wind gave me a fever the third day, so I had
to nurse myself and did not risk exposure again.[70]

A letter to his mother, written on January 16, from Kinshasa, is
filled with pure elation at finding there waiting to greet him, the
English couple, Mr. and Mrs. Adamson, ready to go back upriver
with him to work at Luebo!

Reached Kinshasa yesterday. Dr. Sims seemed pleased to see
me, and then Mr. Adamson and Mrs. Adamson!!! You don't
know how satisfying it is to see a white lady after so many
months of savagery. Adamson has done himself a good
turn, and us, too. His wife is pleasant looking, gentle
and tidy, and reminds me of my Glen Addie friends, Miss
Mary T. and her sister.

Mrs. Adamson keeps house for us four, Dr. Sims and I
making up the number, and she makes other good things
besides food and tea. She has just fixed up the doctor with a
new mosquito bar, and an official inspection of my quarters
was made on pretense of showing me the pretty little
Gleichman baby. I hadn't a pillow case on the little pillow I
brought from home. You see, Shamba Mwana is forgetful,
and I only discovered that he had forgotten to bring it when
he was gone off to sleep in some nook or corner of the
Florida. So, I was reminded of my carelessness by Mrs.
Adamson's coming to me with a pillow case, asking leave to
put it on the pillow.[71]

A letter written while still in Kinshasa adds some revealing
insights into the use of his time:

I am writing out the grammar and vocabulary of the language spoken around Luebo, as far as I have mastered it.

Mr. Adamson improves the waiting time here by making the molds for a brick press, by means of which Luebo is to be built of burnt and pressed brick. Remember, Mr. Adamson has already put through one big job on the Congo, the remounting of the steamer *Pioneer*. His father was a large contractor; built some of the famous Liverpool docks. Mrs. Adamson is making clothes for the bachelor contingent here.

I am well and in excellent spirits. I believe the American Presbyterian Congo Mission is going to do good, and to get started at it before very long, if God wills.[72]

On March 12, Lapsley wrote a letter to his father from Tunduwa (Underhill), the Baptist mission station at Matadi. While in Leopoldville, he had received a letter from the governor general of the Congo Free State at Boma, informing him that the land requested for the mission concession at Luebo had already been granted to someone else. A request for another place in the vicinity could be submitted. As the commissaire of the Kasai District himself had seen the concession originally requested, and had assured the missionaries that it was unclaimed, Lapsley knew that "there must be some mistake or trickery." He decided immediately to proceed to Boma, to discuss the whole matter in person with the governor general.

At Lukunga, on the way to Boma, Lapsley received more disturbing news. Dr. Guiness of the Congo Balolo Mission

Reverend Samuel N. Lapsley shortly before his death at the Swedish Baptist Mission station, Tunduwa, Underhill, one mile downriver from Matadi. Courtesy—Department of History, PCUSA, Montreat, North Carolina.

informed him that their mission was no longer conveniently able to handle transport for the American Presbyterian Congo Mission. Some other arrangement would have to be made for the mission far up in the Kasai to receive needed supplies for carrying on the work.[73]

Lapsley recognized God's leading in bringing him back to the Pool and to the Lower Congo at this very time, to deal with these two basic problems.

It had been less than two years since Lapsley and Sheppard had made the trek up-country, around Stanley Falls to the Pool. The progress in constructing the railroad, made during that time, was truly amazing! Trains were now carrying cargo as far as Mpozo and the tracks extended even beyond that point. Beyond all expectation, Lapsley rejoiced that "within only four years, it will extend all the way to Stanley Pool!"

He concluded his last letter to his father with a description of what he could see through the open doorway of his room, as he wrote. That doorway framed a view of Devil's Caldron at Matadi, the roiling maelstrom of brown water beyond which travel in oceangoing vessels is no longer possible. Blocked by the monstrous barricade of the rugged Crystal Mountains the Congo River makes a right turn here and all the water from eight thousand miles of Upper Congo waterways funnels seaward into this one seething caldron. It's like "no other river on the globe!" marveled Lapsley. He believed that it was "more majestic right at Matadi than as it passes over the cataracts or stretches for miles in width above Stanley Pool."

A brief postscript was added to the last letter written to his father:

> Boma, March 17, 1892—Back from dining with the Governor.
> He was very obliging, only heard my case at 4 p.m., put it
> through, and handed me the letter when we came to dinner.
> Thanked God and took courage! I go back to Matadi
> tomorrow.[74]

The doctor who had given Lapsley his physical examination in the United States, before his acceptance as a missionary by the Executive Committee of Foreign Missions, had reported that he was in good health, well fit for service. He also had warned the young minister of the grave dangers of African climate, to which he replied, "That will not deter me!"

The last episode in Lapsley's life is best described by the missionary who cared for him during his final illness. This was written to his parents by the Reverend K. J. Petersen of the Swedish mission near Matadi:

> It so happened I was here arranging to start building a station for our society, near Matadi, when your son took ill. He seemed to me to be in low health generally, although he said he felt well. He said he had had Black Water Fever several times, but, apart from that, he had good health. Yet he dreaded another such fever, and said several times he wished that "fever would leave him alone."
>
> He went down to Boma and returned. Not feeling very well, he stayed in bed, but made very light of his ailment. . . .
>
> On Sunday morning there was a repetition of hematuria. I got him to bed at once, and applied the usual remedies. . . . Having had a good deal of experience in the sick-room, as well as hospital training, I was asked to take charge of the case, which I did willingly; and, except one night and a few hours of daytime, I spent all my time attending to Mr. Lapsley.

Mr. Petersen reported that Lapsley kept very quiet all the time and did not once mention death until the last day. He did find out that his patient had continually been fearing the worst, having realized for some time that he could go through only a certain number of attacks of that usually fatal phase of malaria. Mr. Petersen continued:

> I had good hopes of his recovery until the early morning of the last day, when I found that the temperature did not fall as low as usual. Instead, it gradually rose, but I still hoped I could check the fever. We tried all we could think of. I had not mentioned my fear to him, but when I told him we wished to try a cold bath, he said, "Yes, and if that doesn't succeed, you will find my will in my bag, and other valuables are on the table. Other instructions I have left with Mr. Whyte."

We tried the cold bath, and brought the temperature down
a good deal. However, it rose again, feeling which, he said:
"It is no use. Bless my father and mother. Please tell them I
go home to be with Jesus, where I wish to meet them. I am
sorry for my poor Mission, but they will find a better man.
Say good-bye to all my relations and friends." After that,
delirium set in, and he soon quietly passed away.[75]

Samuel Lapsley died on Saturday, March 26, 1892. One of the
last things for which he expressed concern was the safe return of
the boy, Shamba Muana, back to Luebo.

The Reverend R. H. C. Graham of the Baptist Missionary
Society conducted the simple service of his burial. He wrote to
Lapsley's parents that their son had been "laid to rest on Sunday
morning in our little cemetery among the trees, down by the riverside, where sleep quite a number of our brethren until He comes."
Those who were present included many missionaries of the Lower
Congo missions which Lapsley had visited, as well as his good
friends, Dr. and Mrs. George Grenfell from the Upper Congo. Also
present were little Shamba Muana, the Bakete chief's son, who had
traveled all the way from Luebo to Matadi with him, and many of
the carriers who had made the overland trip with him from Matadi
to Kinshasa around Stanley Falls. The Reverend Mr. Graham had
an "opportunity of speaking to all of these, and also to his own
mission workmen and school children of the Savior in whom our
dear brother had trusted, and in whose service he had given up his
life for the sake of Africa."[76]

The following is a copy of Lapsley's will:

The year one thousand eight hundred and ninety-two, the
twenty-fourth day of the month of February, I, the under-
signed, Lapsley, Samuel Norvell, Missionary at Luebo, give
and bequeath to my father, Judge James W. Lapsley, of
Anniston, Alabama, United States of America, my English
Bible and my watch, and I further give and bequeath to the
American Presbyterian Congo Mission all other property and
effects of which I may be possessed within the Congo

Lapsley's gravestone and the cemetery at Tunduwa, near Matadi. Courtesy—Mrs. Glenn Murray, Lubbock, Texas.

Independent State, and I hereby name and appoint Sheppard, William and Adamson, George, executors of this my will.
[Signed,] Samuel Norvell Lapsley.[77]

Lapsley's tombstone reads:

SAMUEL NORVELL LAPSLEY
OF THE
AMERICAN PRESBYTERIAN
CONGO MISSION
BORN SELMA, ALABAMA U.S.A.
APRIL 14th 1866
DIED HERE IN GOD'S SERVICE
MARCH 26th 1892

"Too Much Goodness for His Strength"

Lapsley's friend, Dr. Sims, wrote to his parents: "I dearly loved your son and regard him as a real martyr. I warned him to go home, but he wished to complete a definite work before doing that. He had too much goodness for his strength!"

Unlike the English Presbyterian missionary, Dr. Summers, beside whose grave at Tshinyama Lapsley had grieved, "He had no one to carry on what he had begun!" he himself *did* have successors! At first they were few in number, but as the years passed, the work begun by Sheppard and Lapsley grew.

During its final years, throughout the 1950s, the American Presbyterian Congo Mission was the largest Protestant mission in the Belgian Congo. At eleven different mission stations, approximately 170 missionaries were engaged in extensive evangelistic, medical, industrial, and educational programs.

When the Upper Congo-Kasai segment of the Presbyterian Church of Zaire, carefully nurtured to birth by the mission, assumed autonomy on November 2, 1959, it had a membership of 70,000 baptized Christians, 300 ordained pastors, 1,100 evangelists, and 3,109 places of regular worship. On that day, the American Presbyterian Congo Mission founded by Lapsley and Sheppard,

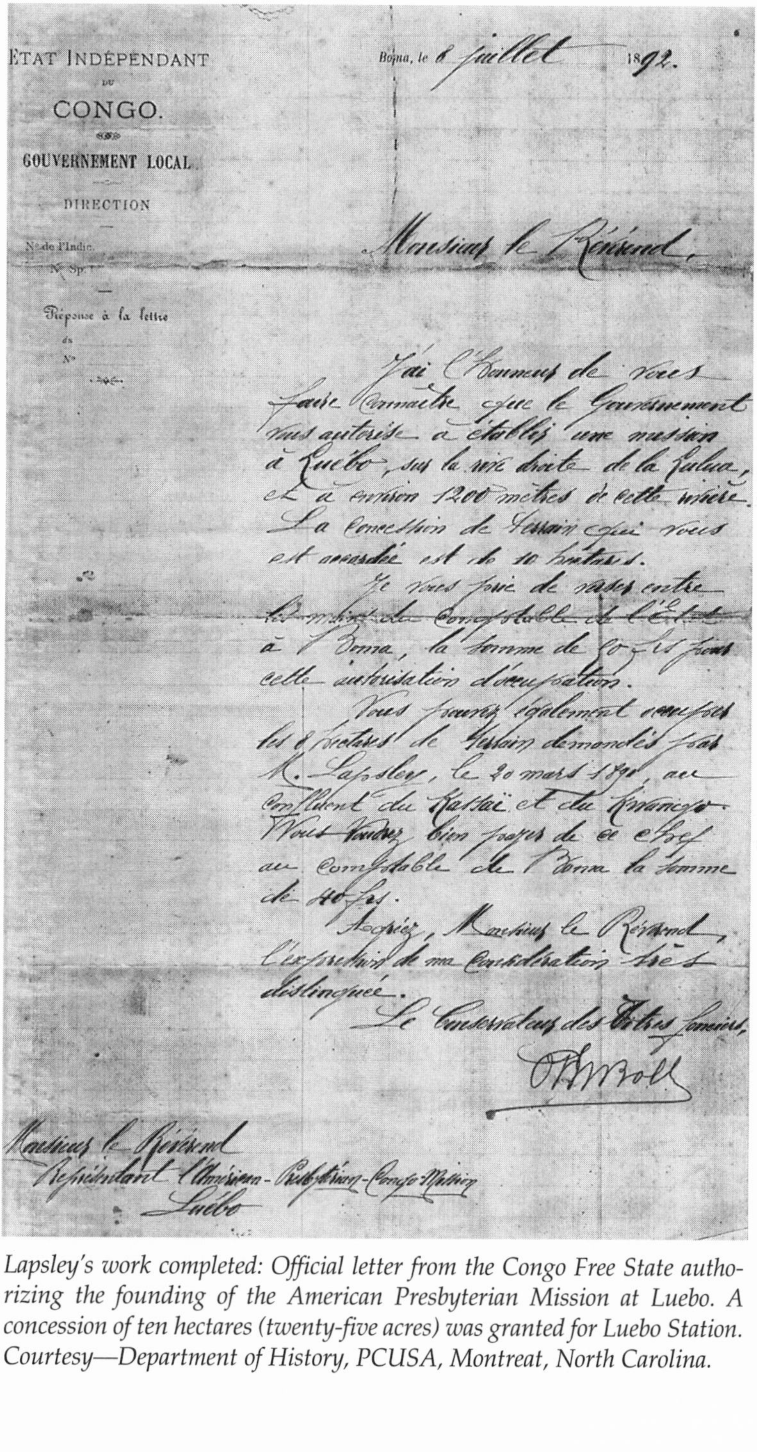

ETAT INDÉPENDANT
DU
CONGO.
GOUVERNEMENT LOCAL
DIRECTION
N° de l'Indic.
N° Sp.
Réponse à la lettre
du
N°

Boma, le 8 juillet 1892.

Monsieur le Révérend,

J'ai l'honneur de vous faire connaître que le Gouvernement vous autorise à établir une mission à Luebo, sur la rive droite de la Lulua, et à environ 1200 mètres de cette rivière. La concession de terrain qui vous est accordée est de 10 hectares.

Je vous prie de verser entre les mains du Comptable de l'Etat à Boma, la somme de 50 frs pour cette autorisation d'occupation.

Vous pourrez également occuper les 8 hectares de terrain demandés par M. Lapsley, le 20 mars 1890, au confluent du Kassaï et du Kwango. Vous voudrez bien payer de ce chef au Comptable de Boma la somme de 40 frs.

Agréez, Monsieur le Révérend, l'expression de ma considération très distinguée.

Le Conservateur des Titres fonciers,

[signature]

Monsieur le Révérend
Représentant l'American Presbyterian Congo Mission
Luebo

Lapsley's work completed: Official letter from the Congo Free State authorizing the founding of the American Presbyterian Mission at Luebo. A concession of ten hectares (twenty-five acres) was granted for Luebo Station. Courtesy—Department of History, PCUSA, Montreat, North Carolina.

ceased to exist and in a solemn ceremony at Kananga, the indigenous Presbyterian Church of Zaire came into being. At the first General Assembly, the new Church voted officially to retain the denominational name of its founding mission. Civil status (*personalite civile*) was granted the new Church by Belgian Congo authorities on March 5, 1960.

On June 10, 1960, Belgium reluctantly granted independence to its one colony, even though there had been no preparation for self-rule. In God's wise and gracious providence, the new Church entered the new era organized to make its own official decisions.

Since the early 1960s, a brutal, repressive thirty-year-long dictatorial regime has stubbornly resisted growing popular pressure for democratic reform. This regime is characterized by cold-blooded elimination of opposition, arbitrary arrests by a dictator-controlled military machine, deliberate "ethnic cleansing," the complete collapse of a once-viable infrastructure, total economic breakdown, near-zero employment, a gross national product of only 10 percent, and resulting widespread famine and starvation.

In spite of the agonizing duration of this fearful state of non-government, suffering and turmoil, the Presbyterian Church of Zaire has continued to grow.

The Upper Congo-Kasai segment of the Church, where it was founded, combined with its sister church in Kinshasa and the Lower Congo, had in 1992 a total membership of 1,253,632.[78]

Shortly before his crucifixion, our Lord stated: "Unless a kernel of wheat falls to the ground and dies, it remains only a single seed. But if it dies, it produces many seeds" (John 12:24).

Praise God for this one "grain of wheat" that was the brief, triumphant life of Samuel N. Lapsley!

Notes

1. *Life and Letters of Samuel Norvell Lapsley* (Richmond, Va.: Whittet and Shepperson, Printers, Tenth and Main Streets, 1893), 96.
2. Ibid., 11.
3. Ibid., 13.
4. Ibid., 15.
5. Ibid., 16–17.

6. Ibid., 18–19.

7. Ibid., 21.

8. William H. Sheppard, *Presbyterian Pioneers in Congo* (Richmond, Va.: Presbyterian Committee of Publication, 1917), 15–18.

9. Ibid., 19.

10. Stanley Shaloff, *Reform in Leopold's Congo* (Richmond, Va.: John Knox Press, 1970), 20.

11. Ibid., 31–33.

12. *Presbyterian Pioneers in Congo,* 21.

13. *Life and Letters of Samuel Norvell Lapsley,* 36.

14. Ibid., 37–38.

15. Ibid., 38–39.

16. Ibid., 40–43.

17. Ibid., 43–45.

18. Ibid., 46.

19. Ibid., 47–48.

20. Ibid., 49.

21. Ibid., 50.

22. Ibid.

23. Ibid., 53–54.

24. *Reform in Leopold's Congo,* 22.

25. *Life and Letters of Samuel N. Lapsley,* 56.

26. Ibid., 57.

27. Ibid., 58.

28. Ibid., 61–62.

29. Ibid., 62.

30. Ibid., 65.

31. Ibid.

32. Ibid., 68.

33. Ibid.

34. Ibid., 70–71.

35 Ibid., 71.

36. Ibid., 72–73.

37. Ibid., 74.

38. Ibid., 75–76.

39. Ibid., 77–78.

40. Ibid., 78.

41. Ibid., 79.

42. Ibid., 80.
43. Ibid., 80–81.
44. Ibid., 82.
45. Ibid., 81–82.
46. Ibid., 96.
47. Ibid., 85.
48. Ibid., 97.
49. Ibid., 83.
50. Ibid.
51. Ibid.
52. *Presbyterian Pioneers in Congo*, 75–76.
53. Ibid., 64–65.
54. *Life and Letters of Samuel N. Lapsley*, 88.
55. Ibid., 89.
56. Ibid., 91, 99.
57. Ibid., 100.
58. *Presbyterian Pioneers in Congo*, 67–68.
59. *Life and Letters of Samuel N. Lapsley*, 92–93.
60. Ibid., 99.
61. Ibid., 101.
62. Ibid., 102.
63. Ibid.
64. Ibid., 104.
65. Ibid.
66. Ibid., 105.
67. Ibid.
68. *Presbyterian Pioneers in Congo*, 80.
69. Ibid., 82.
70. *Life and Letters of Samuel N. Lapsley*, 106–07.
71. Ibid., 108.
72. Ibid., 108–09.
73. Ibid., 109.
74. Ibid.
75. Ibid., 111–13.
76. Ibid., 113–14.
77. Ibid., 114.
78. 1991–1992 Statistics, Evangelism, Presbyterian Church of Zaire.

Part II

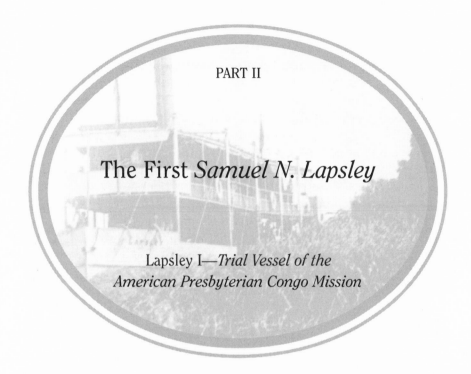

PART II

The First *Samuel N. Lapsley*

Lapsley I—*Trial Vessel of the
American Presbyterian Congo Mission*

The Need for a Steamer

DID LAPSLEY'S SUDDEN, UNEXPECTED DEATH FROM THE
blackwater fever jeopardize the existence of the American
Presbyterian Congo Mission? On the contrary, the very brevity and
brilliance of his missionary service kindled a glowing spark in the
home church.

Lapsley's and Sheppard's careful search for the best site for their
first mission station had kept them on the Zaire river-highways for
nine long months. Lapsley's visit up the main channel of the river
to visit Dr. George Grenfell was much more prolonged than he had
anticipated; he was detained from July 29 to September 23,
awaiting a steamer to take him downriver to Kinshasa. This experience was the first to make him realize the important role that

61

mission steamers played in making travel possible.

The two missionaries' hazardous experience of struggling up the Kwango and Kwilu tributaries in a dugout canoe, only to be met by furious, open hostility, forced them to bring their exploration of this area to a close. Because of the belligerent refusal of the local tribes to let them set foot upon their beaches, it proved impossible to procure food for their hungry oarsmen. How much safer were the decks of a river steamer that could outdistance the long *pirogues* filled with warriors!

It was on a state steamer, the *Florida*, that Sheppard and Lapsley finally reached their destination, Luebo, on April 18, 1891, at the confluence of the Lulua and Luebo Rivers. This vessel lacked the power even to tow their dugout; it had to be left at Kinshasa, along with half their cargo of critically needed supplies. A mission-owned vessel would be the only solution to meet the missionaries' need for supplies for the work and to maintain their own well-being.

The Peace, *constructed in London, reassembled at Stanley Pool by Dr. George Grenfell, Baptist Missionary Society. This was the steamer on which he did his famous explorations of the Upper Congo. Courtesy—Musée Royale de l'Afrique, Tervuren, Belgique.*

On March 10, 1891, Lapsley wrote to his father, "I think we shall suffer delays until we do our own transport with a Presbyterian mission steamer."[1]

Three other missions already had steamers. The Baptist Missionary Society had its *Peace*, built on the Thames in England, taken apart and shipped in eight hundred crates to Matadi, then carried on the backs of porters around the cataracts up to Stanley Pool. Because of the deaths of the first three engineers sent to assemble the steamer at Stanley Pool, it was Dr. George Grenfell himself who literally "prayed it together," using only inexperienced native help.[2]

The American Baptist Mission had its *Henry Reed*, first constructed in England for the Livingston Inland Mission. Henry M. Stanley rented it in 1889 to transport his famous Emin Pasha Relief Expedition as far as Stanley Falls.[3]

The *Pioneer* of the Congo Balolo Mission had been assembled by a young Scottish machinist named George D. Adamson. It was Adamson and his bride who were the first missionaries to join Sheppard at Luebo following Lapsley's death.[4]

If other missions had, by the grace of God, surmounted the obstacles presented by the formidable geographical barrier of the Crystal Mountains and the fearsome cataracts of the Zaire River, surely the American Presbyterian Congo Mission could do it, too! Now, especially, there was new hope, for a 250-mile-long, narrow-gauge railroad was under construction to bypass the impassable stretch of river between Matadi and Kinshasa.

Pennies and Dimes to the Rescue

In 1892 the Executive Committee of Foreign Missions of the Presbyterian Church in the United States sent two new couples to join Sheppard and the Adamsons in the work at Luebo. They were the Reverend and Mrs. Arthur Rowbotham and a pharmacist with medical experience, Dr. D. W. Snyder, and his wife. During their brief stay in London, en route to the Congo Free State, they procured information on the probable costs of providing a steamer for the American Presbyterian Congo Mission. Mr. Rowbotham wrote:

We very greatly need a small steamer, as other missions
have, and pray our Father to give us one. The trading companies carry us and our goods, it is true, but conditionally upon
their not having sufficient cargo for the trip. . . . This is a
question of grave importance. We cannot use the boats of the
Baptist Societies, because they have [Upper] Congo [River]
work only, not going up the [Kasai] tributaries as we do; and
at best we and our goods are not carried from the Pool
directly to our station, but as the traders go in search of ivory
and rubber up one stream and down another, so we and our
goods are delayed for weeks and perhaps months.

To find out what could be done in the way of getting a boat,
Mr. Snyder and I went to see Messrs. Yarrow, who built
Stanley's boat for the purpose of navigating the Congo. We
can buy a boat fifty feet long, with eight feet beam, drawing
about ten inches of water and carrying five tons, made in
sections, for about $5,000; this is a good outside estimate. To
put it on the Upper Congo will cost about $5,000 more—in
all $10,000. . . . Let the Sunday Schools do this. Why not
name the boat THE LAPSLEY?[5]

A new church-wide project aimed particularly at children was
announced in the January 1893 issue of *The Missionary*. Children
were called to "raise $10,000 for the purpose of building a boat to
be used for carrying supplies to our missionaries in Africa, to
travel up and down the Congo River and to be called *The Samuel
N. Lapsley*."[6] The February 1893 issue continued:

So, we intend to have a Congo Steamboat Company and the
children shall have shares in it. Every child, or every class in
the Sunday School that sends $1.00 for the Congo Boat, will
receive a certificate and hold a share in the steamboat.[7]

This same issue featured a little African-American girl from
West Virginia:

Her teacher writes us that this girl has been untiring in her
efforts to get a dollar for the Congo Boat. She has earned her

money by picking up [cow] chips, hunting eggs for which she gets a few cents for every dozen she finds; collecting and destroying caterpillar eggs from apple trees; sweeping, combing hair, and at last, by real self-denial, in parting with one of her beloved books to a companion who offered to buy it.[8]

It also included one of the monthly listings of the names of donors and the amount given to "The Congo Boat Fund":

Pearl Gatherers, Cleveland, Tenn.—$29.55

Miss M. E. White's Sunday School class, Fancy Hill, Va.—$6.28

Wigston Sunday School (col,d), Pickaway, W. Va.—$4.40

Miss M. E. McCampbell, Goliad, Texas—.25¢

Rev. Walter Boxendale, W. Norwood, London—$3.00

St. George's Presbyterian Church, Bardesbury, London—$5.00

Sunday School of Crescent Hill Church, Louisville, Ky.—$51.00

[Sub-total] $99.48—Previously received, $220.50.

Total received to date, $319.98.[9]

Adamson urged: "We cannot have a large mission without a steamer! Now it is for the children to say how soon that steamer shall be bought. Come, Children, one and all, let us have the steamer soon!"[10]

It was not the joyful giving of the children that decided when the boat would be constructed. In one year they did succeed in raising that $10,000. But there were other factors involved which had to be considered.

In 1895 Dr. S. H. Chester, the secretary of Foreign Missions of the Presbyterian Church, U.S., wrote a letter to all who had given to the fund for financing the construction of the mission steamer. He explained to the children in particular:

> We have found out that it would cost us about twice $10,000 to build such a boat as would be useful to us on the Congo and that the care of the boat and the hiring of men to run it would cost a great deal more than it now costs to get other people to carry our missionaries and their supplies.

He explained that the $10,000 already given had been safely placed in a trust fund.[11]

Mr. Robert Whyte concurred with the decision of the Executive Committee of Foreign Missions to postpone the construction of the mission boat; he felt that the mission should wait until its staff was larger. Dr. Snyder and the Reverend Mr. Sheppard also felt that it would be a mistake to build at that time.

Three years passed in which the missionaries of the American Presbyterian Congo Mission continued to struggle with the difficult problem of transportation.

Cries of frustration were again voiced in 1898, this time with increasing desperation and intensity. The transportation problem had become critical. Even during the season of high waters, commercial steamers did not bother to go the few additional miles up the Lulua River to reach Luebo station. They unceremoniously dumped mission cargo at Bena Makima on the main channel of the Kasai River and went their merry way. For five or six months at a time during the dry season, the mission staff went without receiving supplies of food, barter goods, or mail. On June 1, 1898, Dr. Snyder wrote that news had come that boxes and mail had been left at Bena Makima, seventy miles overland. Seventy miles in a civilized country is no problem, but in Africa it meant another week of waiting while a caravan of no less than eighty men had to be hired and paid to walk to Bena Makima and return with the loads on their heads to Luebo. On June 9, word came that another one hundred cases were waiting there. This time two carriers per box were required, for heavier loads were tied to strong poles that rested on the shoulders of two men. That meant hiring and paying two hundred men, and for the missionary men, worst of all, weeks away from the real work they had come to do! Many times the long-awaited cases of food supplies had been emptied of their contents, as they had sat so many months in the warehouse at Kinshasa.[12]

An anguished cry was also heard from Dr. Morrison who wrote from Luebo on November 17, 1898:

> We have not had a steamer at Luebo since *March*, so about a week ago, when the whistle blew, I rushed down to the beach, anxious to get the mail and much-needed barter goods. Finding the captain, I asked, "Any mail for the Mission?" Answer: "No, it was put off at Lusambo and is coming to Luebo overland." My heart now fairly sank within me, but I ventured to ask one more question, "Have you any good news for the Mission?" Answer: "None!"[13]

The last news had been received in April as the Spanish-American War threatened. The little band of isolated missionaries were desperate for news of the war from their homeland. Morale was at a low ebb!

Construction and Dedication of the Steamer

A "hurting" mission was greatly saddened in 1898 by the deaths of both Mrs. Adamson and Mrs. Snyder. But now new recruits were on the way! By 1900, the staff numbered twelve, six of whom were African American and six Caucasian. Their deep frustration over their transport problem in the fall of 1898 led them to send Dr. Snyder to England with instructions to consult with the executive committee and make all arrangements to have the steamer constructed and sent out. On his way downriver, in Kinshasa, Dr. Snyder met a newly arrived young recruit, the Reverend Lachlan C. Vass Jr. The two discussed fully the problems involved in reassembling the steamer on Stanley Pool. At Dr.

Snyder's insistence, Mr. Vass agreed to undertake the reconstruction work when the steamer arrived.

> Dr. Snyder then continued his journey to England, and there,
> with the assistance of Mr. Robert Whyte, contacted several
> ship building firms who were familiar with the construction
> of river steamers for tropical river navigation. These tenta-
> tive plans were sent to the Executive Committee in Nashville
> who decided that the steamer could be constructed to better
> advantage in America than in England. The carrying out of
> this work was then taken out of the hands of Dr. Snyder, and
> after a short visit to his family in America, he returned to the
> Congo. The steamer was then contracted for, to be built by
> the William R. Trigg Co. of Richmond, Virginia. It was a stern
> wheel boat of 70 foot length, 12 foot beam, 32 ft. depth and 1
> foot 1 inch draught. It had a hold capacity of 1,450 cubic feet,
> one upper deck cabin for the captain, and two cabins for
> passengers on the lower deck.[14]

It was a happy day, when the news finally came that the
Presbyterian "powers that be" had decided that it was time to
provide a steamer for their African mission!

On August 23, 1899, the beloved family church paper, the
Christian Observer, addressed a letter to "Dear Young Readers":

> Vigorous efforts are now being made for the speedy
> construction of the "Congo Boat," for the use of our mission-
> aries on the Congo River in Africa.

> The money for the building of this boat was contributed by
> you or your older brothers and sisters a few years ago. Some
> difficulties arose about the building of the boat, and it has
> been delayed. The need of it is now greatly felt, and Dr.
> Snyder is in this country with a view of having it built at
> once. Our mission is situated in a very fortunate locality,
> where it has access to a great many native Africans who
> have never heard the Gospel, and who are not prejudiced
> against it. But this places it out of the usual line of river
> travel on the Congo; and especially when the water is low in

the Lulua River, on which our mission station at Luebo is situated, the ordinary riverboats do not come to it for six months of the year. A special boat is needed.

The money that was contributed for this boat ($10,000) is still in hand and will be used to build it. But the Foreign Mission Committee finds that several thousand dollars will be needed to transport it to Africa and to carry it up the Congo above the falls, and have it put up again.[15]

Certificates issued for this additional amount were called "Launching Certificates" and were presented to donors for any contribution from ten cents upward. Dimes contributed by the children began to roll in just as the pennies had so freely in 1893. The needed sum of six thousand dollars was soon raised and the contract signed for the construction of the mission boat.

On June 23, 1900, the original *Samuel N. Lapsley* was dedicated at the William R. Trigg Ship Yards on the James River in Richmond, Virginia. All around the mission vessel were the hulks of many war vessels under construction for fighting in the Spanish-American War, then in progress.

The day after the dedication, the *Richmond Times* gave thirty-seven column inches of space to the unusual story. Six rows of headlines, each in a different style or size of type announced:

THE LAPSLEY HAS BEEN DEDICATED
Unique Exercises Held at the Trigg Yards
MANY WITNESSES
Immense Crowd Present and Saw the Novel Ceremony
Performed
THE GIFT OF THE CHILDREN

Dr. S. H. Chester, Secretary of the Foreign Mission Board
in an Eloquent Address Tells How the
Movement to Build the Steamer Was
Started in Africa

Dr. Robert P. Kerr, chairman of the board, closed the ceremony by wishing the boat "God-speed, as a white-winged messenger of peace to Africa." He referred to the *Lapsley* as "a dove born in an eagle's nest" because of the steel vessels all around it being prepared for battle action.

After the ceremony, the builders placed in the hands of the Reverend J. E. Cook, one of the Richmond commissioners, thousands of the steel disks made in perforating the steel plates of the boat for the insertion of rivets. Mr. Cook sent these to the office of the mission board in Nashville, suggesting that they be sold as souvenirs of the boat—a "bright idea" for adding to "The Congo Boat Fund."[16]

The *South Western Press* on July 19, 1900, reported:

> The Congo mission boat, *Samuel N. Lapsley*, which was launched at the Trigg Yards Saturday, June 23, was registered at the Richmond Custom House on June 27. This will, therefore, be the *Lapsley's* home port. The mission craft . . . will fly the American flag. It is rare that a certificate of registry is first unsealed in a foreign country, but the *Lapsley's* papers will be delivered to her officers in Africa.[17]

On August 20, the same publication announced: "The Congo River missionary boat, *Samuel N. Lapsley*, was shipped from the shipyards of William R. Trigg Company last week, and is now on the way to Africa."[18] The original *Lapsley*, disassembled and crated for shipment to Stanley Pool, was on its way at last!

The Right Man for the Job

Were not the heroes of the ancient Norse sea sagas stern, towering warrior giants? What is a happy-spirited, nimble, feisty, rather short-statured preacher doing in this African river saga? Watch him, for like Queen Esther, he proved to be the man "come to the kingdom for such a time as this!" He would be the one to supervise the reassembling of the original *Samuel N. Lapsley*.

In Lachlan Cumming Vass Jr. were combined the faith and fortitude of his French-Huguenot Fontaine-Maury grandmother and the

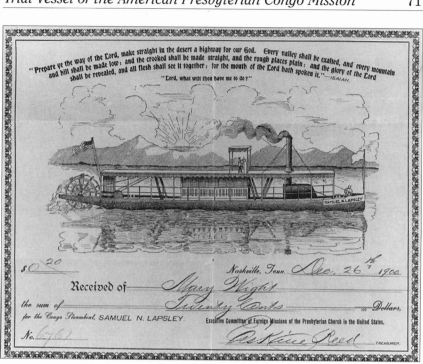

Certificate issued to donor, showing drawing of the first Samuel N. Lapsley, *built by William R. Trigg Co. of Richmond, Virginia, in April 1900. Length, seventy feet; breadth, twelve feet; depth, three feet six inches; draught, one foot one inch. Capacity of hold, 1,450 cubic feet; speed, ten miles per hour. Courtesy—Department of History, PCUSA, Montreat, North Carolina.*

canny, capable sturdiness of his Scottish Cumming-Vass grandfather. James Boswell, writing in 1775 about his tour to the Hebrides with Dr. Samuel Johnson, tells about one of their two guides, Lauchlan Vass, a hardy Highlander, who helped them most agreeably with his sturdy "ponies" through the snowdrifts. "Lachlan," a Gaelic name, has been a family name for generations.[19]

    Mr. Vass received an excellent education at the famous Pantops Academy in Virginia and at Davidson College. It was while he was a student at Davidson that he committed his life to Christ for full-time service in response to a message given by Robert E. Speer, then a student at Princeton Seminary. After graduation from Davidson

Rev. Lachlan C. Vass II, who reassembled and captained the first Samuel N. Lapsley. Courtesy— Department of History, PCUSA, Montreat, North Carolina.

in 1894, Vass entered Columbia Presbyterian Theological Seminary (when it was still in Columbia, South Carolina) to prepare for the ministry and possible missionary service.

While a student at the seminary, he was also enrolled in courses at the University of South Carolina to qualify as a member of the USC football team. Extremely athletic, the 125-pound, 5-foot 2-inch athlete who had played football in college, now became one of the first "ringers" for the South Carolina varsity. Being very fast on his feet, he, as the quarterback, carried the football, breaking away from the offensive wedge and outrunning the opposing players. (At the age of sixty, he would outrun his eighteen-year-old son, Lachlan III, in a footrace!)

Following his graduation from seminary in 1897, he held pastorates in Spartanburg, South Carolina, and Matthews, North Carolina, where he was when he received his summons from the Executive Committee of Foreign Missions to serve in the Congo Free State.

It was Mr. Vass's physical stamina and a native quality of dogged persistence and drive that would keep him going during the long months of grueling labor ahead, necessary for reassembling the *Lapsley*. More important still was his natural gift for careful, demanding accuracy. His son, Lachlan, recalls that very often his father had his Hamilton railroad watch set to Greenwich time by his jeweler, in order that his church services would start exactly on time. He also had a keen sense of proper function and a theoretical understanding of mechanics that enabled him to meet the demands of the complicated engineering task of putting together the Presbyterian mission paddle wheeler.

Staff of Luebo station, American Presbyterian Congo Mission in 1900. Front row, left to right: Rev. Joseph E. Phipps, Rev. William H. Sheppard, and Rev. Henry P. Hawkins. Back row: Rev. William M. Morrison and Rev. Lachlan C. Vass II. Courtesy—Department of History, PCUSA, Philadelphia, Pennsylvania.

Dr. Morrison, in his daily diary, gave his first impressions of the energetic twenty-eight year old who had joined the mission staff:

Friday, March 10, 1899
At 1 p.m. a [boat's] whistle blew and we rushed down to meet Mr. Vass and were not disappointed.

In appearance, he has . . . light hair, sandy and scattering beard of recent growth, medium size but well built. He has been most fortunate—no fever yet, a good passage, and none of the horrors of the caravan route and the perhaps worse horrors of Stanley Pool, all of which we of former days so dreaded [before construction of the narrow gauge railroad around the cataracts].

Mr. Vass knows (?) plenty just now; but he will *know less* as he becomes better informed!

Saturday, March 12, 1899
Vass seems to have a decidedly mechanical turn and will, I think, be the man for the *boat*.[20]

The native people of Central Africa have an uncanny ability to perceive character and cleverly identify it with a very accurate, "telling" name. Noting young Vass's abounding energy, quick movements, and early involvement in the station work, they gave him the Bantu name, *Malu Malu*, meaning "one who stays busy with many responsibilities."

Such was the man chosen of God to launch the dedicated riverboat ministry of the American Presbyterian Congo Mission.

Reassembling the Original *Samuel N. Lapsley*

"With God's help, I will do my best!" Lachlan Vass had replied when officially requested to undertake the reconstruction of the *Lapsley*. That help became evident as he tackled the initial task of overseeing the unloading of the crated paddle wheeler from the hold of the oceangoing steamer. The heavy crates of machinery and steel plates filled more than five of the narrow-gauge railroad cars. How grateful young Vass was for that tiny, barely adequate railroad! At least he did not have to superintend the manhandling of all those crates overland, as earlier mission steamers for

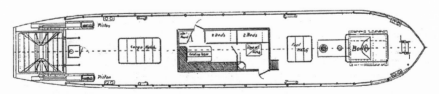

This deck plan of the first Samuel N. Lapsley *shows the location of the boiler at the bow and the engine at the stern of the steamer. The wheelhouse was above the boiler.* Courtesy—Christian Observer, *December 27, 1899, page 17.*

upper-river navigation had been transported.

European engineering companies in Leopoldville were invited to make bids for reassembling the *Lapsley*, but the bids were too high to be considered. The job simply had to be done under missionary direction, with inexperienced labor.[21]

Mr. Vass's own account of how he tackled the primary task of unloading the flatcars shows how innovative he was in overcoming difficult logistic problems. On November 11, 1900, he wrote, describing his initial efforts:

> The boat has arrived at Leopoldville. It made a little over five carloads. The cars, though, are not as large as ours in America. It took me about seven or eight days of very hard work to get it unloaded and taken down to the river where I have erected a slip-way on which to build. We have no conveniences here for discharging heavy loads, so it was a little puzzling at first to tell how to remove the loads, quite a number of which weighed a ton and over. The usual weight of our loads is about 100 pounds. I secured a good many old rice sacks, and had them stuffed tightly with grass. These were spread around on the edge of the cars and on the ground at the side to make a soft place. Two strong pieces of timber were then laid on top of these. A long rope was tied around the box at each end, and a crowd of workmen would slide the box from its place high on the car. Its fall was effectively broken by the springing of the sacks and thus all the breakable parts were successfully unloaded.
>
> Everything was then spread out on the ground in rows that the various pieces might be checked off by the railroad officials and received by myself for the mission. Then came an equally hard job of moving everything down to the river, about 400 or 500 yards away. All the heavy cases with parts of machinery, etc., in them were opened and the contents could then be easily carried by the workers. The engines and heavier pieces had to be dragged along on rollers by main force. The boiler, weighing about 4 1/2 tons, was the most difficult piece to unload, but after a good deal of hard work and shouting at the workers to pull harder at a critical

moment, it was safely landed about 30 feet from the track, where it now lies. It will stay there until I can muster up courage enough to tackle it again and carry it to the river. Mr. Morgan, of the Congo Bololo [sic] Mission was with me most of the time, giving his personal aid and that of his men. If all goes well, I hope to lay down the first keel-plate on Wednesday, November 14, [1899].[22]

Many difficulties were encountered in the reconstruction work. Labor was plentiful, but only entirely untrained native help was available. Most of the workmen had never so much as driven a nail. Now they had to be taught how to rivet the plates of the hull together, in such a way as to assure a watertight vessel. Several West Coast men from Sierra Leone were hired to act as supervisors over groups of local workers. These coast men had been trained for this kind of technical work by English missionaries working in Sierra Leone.

It took four months to complete the reconstruction of the *Lapsley* and ready the steamer for its maiden voyage of approximately nine hundred miles upriver to Luebo.

Voyages of the Original *Lapsley*

In the second issue (July 1, 1901) of the *Kasai Herald*, the English language publication of the American Presbyterian Congo Mission, Captain Vass publicly thanked

. . . the Congo State authorities at Leopoldville for the many favors shown us while reconstructing the steamer. Monsieur Costermans, the Inspector of the State, gave us every assistance possible and in many ways assisted us over difficulties that otherwise would have caused much and serious delay.[23]

The completed steamer's first venture out into the deep waters of the mighty river was what the captain called "a pleasure cruise" across Stanley Pool to Brazzaville. Aboard for this trip were the first ladies to be passengers, Mrs. Snyder with baby Anna, and her friend

First Lapsley *under way on the Kasai River. Courtesy—Department of History, PCUSA, Montreat, North Carolina.*

Mrs. Mallet. A visit to the Kinshasa Customs House provided the necessary permit for crossing over to the French side. Their visit was described as "a pleasant evening walking through the beautiful mango-lined boulevards, with Mrs. Snyder and her baby riding in a jinrikisha." Mr. Greshoff, the genial head of the Dutch Company, where the *Lapsley* had docked, served them a delightful tea in his handsome private office. Weather for the excursion was ideal and the steamer was pronounced a great success.[24]

Future journeys of the *Lapsley* by no means resembled that first cruise across the placid waters of Stanley Pool. On the first upriver journey, the engines broke down and a full day of hard work was necessary to get them in running order again.

Since the first *Lapsley's* records were lost in the capsizing two years later, it is necessary to rely on personal accounts for information. Events, as retold by Captain Vass, give some idea of the difficulties he encountered:

> The [first] journey up the Congo, Kasai and Lulua rivers was begun with a full cargo of sorely needed supplies for the

Mission. The rivers of the Congo at that time were uncharted
and navigation across and around the unending sand banks
was accomplished largely by sight. . . . There were times of
failure to see aright, so the *Lapsley* was the victim quite a
number of times of those provoking obstructions.[25]

Experience taught the captain to watch for a peculiar line on the
surface of the water, which indicated where a sandbank was hidden.
Such extreme vigilance did not, however, prevent groundings.

Whenever the steamer became lodged on a sandbank, the
woodchoppers (who cut wood every night in the forests for the
journey the next day) were put out into the shallow water to push.
With the anchor planted ahead, the straining workmen chanted in
unison, pushing while the engines churned full speed in reverse.
This usually floated the vessel again. Sometimes, however, that
sudden, jarring bump, accompanied by a loud grating, scraping
sound, initiated a very difficult situation. The steamer remained
stuck for several days and local villages had to be visited in order
to buy extra food for the crew, which numbered from thirty to forty.

Dr. William M. Morrison's description of the arrival on May 13,
1901, of the long-awaited mission steamer is a classic in the annals
of the American Presbyterian Congo Mission:

We believe this will always be chronicled as one of the red-
letter days of our Mission, for today the *S. N. Lapsley*
arrived. A courier had come in last night after dark
informing us that she would be in today. This morning,
word was quickly passed from village to village. Gladness
seemed to thrill the hearts of us all, missionary and people
alike. By ten o'clock the crowds began to assemble at the
beach. By twelve o'clock these had grown to perhaps two
thousand or more. One o'clock came and two. We had
placed two fleet-footed boys on a high hill overlooking the
river for a great distance. At half-past two these came
running and shouting. We knew the *Lapsley* had been
sighted. There was a grand rush for the best positions on the
beach. Three large banners had been prepared bearing the
words, "Welcome," "*S. N. Lapsley*," and "Admiral Vass."
Grouped around Miss Thomas and Mrs. Sheppard was a

large choir prepared to send up songs of praise and thanks-
giving. Messrs. Sheppard and Hawkins were on hand ready
to fire an admiral's salute. Within a few minutes after the
alarm was given, as every eye was strained on the bend in
the river, suddenly the *Lapsley* shot into full view! Instantly,
a great shout burst from the wildly enthusiastic crowd. She
drew nearer and nearer, steaming her way slowly against
the swift current. Soon the guns began to fire, a friendly
trader on the other side of the river responded, the choir
began to sing, and the hurrahs echoed from side to side of
the deep gorge in which the river runs. We sighted
"Admiral" Vass on the bridge, and we knew all was well. In
a few minutes the *S. N. Lapsley* lay anchored at the beach,
and we all rushed on board to welcome the "Admiral," and
to congratulate him upon the great work he had accomplished. For never before in the history of this country had a
steamer been rebuilt and actually brought a thousand miles
into the interior by a man who had previously had no experience in such work.

We just felt that the Lord had indeed been most gracious. He
had not only sent the boat, but had sent the man to build
and to run her.

After a few words of welcome on the steamer we proceeded
to the church, and there had a praise service, thanking God
for His mercy and goodness.[26]

The *Lapsley* began the second upriver journey on July 27, 1901,
carrying a large cargo for Luebo and Ibanji stations. The state had
also turned over to Captain Vass twelve bags of mail to be delivered
to government and commercial posts along the main stream of the
river and it largest tributary, the Kasai.

Nine days out of Leopoldville, a serious accident occurred. The
rudder was broken on one of the hidden sandbanks, leaving the
Lapsley in midstream, without means of accurate steering, at a
point where large rocks extended into the river on both sides. It
took some clever maneuvering with the engines to avoid the rocks
and anchor safely in a sandy cove.

This narrow escape that Captain Vass had because of the broken rudder is best described in his own words:

> Leopoldville on Stanley Pool, the nearest place where the rudder could be repaired, was 500 or more miles downriver. We *must* go there as soon as possible!
>
> A crew of eleven good paddlers was selected from the steamer's crew to man the long canoe. This was equipped with sufficient food and other necessary supplies for the trip down. Dr. D. W. Snyder, our only passenger, was left in charge of the steamer. The broken rudder was also loaded and we were off.
>
> Arriving at Mushie, the confluence of the Fimi River flowing in from Lake Leopold II, and the Kasai, we found the currents swift and whirling. A strong wind blowing up stream made the passage even more dangerous.
>
> Attempting to pass this point, the large canoe was swamped and capsized. I, with all my crew, found myself fully clothed and with shoes on, struggling for life amid treacherous currents, with waves beating into my face. I first attempted to swim to the point jutting out where the two rivers came together. Several of my native crew succeeded in making it to this point, but two were drowned. I was swept past the point by the strong current into a broad expanse of swiftly flowing water, formed by the merging rivers. Changing my course, I attempted to swim back and reach the opposite side of the river, which was now the nearer point to reach.
>
> I was soon in rough waters and racing currents, strangled by beating waves, with my strength giving out. Realizing that I would soon be totally exhausted and sink beneath the muddy Kasai water, a cry went up from my heart, "Lord, save me!"
>
> Almost immediately a large felt pillow from the wrecked canoe was washed near enough for me to reach out and grab it. This was thrust quickly under my arm and at once

became a buoyant life preserver. It kept me afloat until a large iron boat from a government post several miles below that spot, saw us and rescued us from certain death.

As we stood in the large boat, exhausted, coughing out all the muddy Kasai water, one of the oarsmen cried, "See, the Book of God!" Our rescuers paddled toward it and indeed it was my Bible, which had been packed in my tin trunk. That Bible and a small package of Bible studies tied in a bundle were all that was ever rescued from the trunk. So God, in a sore time of need, heard our prayers, saved our lives and gave us again His commission to "Go into all the world and preach the Gospel to every creature."

The canoe, with the rudder still miraculously afloat in it, was retrieved. The journey downriver to Leopoldville was continued, the rudder repaired, and returned to its mother ship, which had waited three long weeks for this essential, repaired part.[27]

While Captain Vass was gone, smallpox had broken out among the crew of the stranded steamer, but Dr. Snyder's skilled care prevented any deaths among them. One of the things which the captain was to get in Leopoldville and bring back for the doctor was a supply of smallpox vaccine. On his return, however, he requested Dr. Snyder not to apply the vaccine to any of his oarsmen's strong "rowing arms" until they got back to Luebo!

After the close call of the second voyage, the third one, made in November 1901, was uneventful. Miss Althea Brown, one of the new African-American recruits, wrote:

The voyage on the *Lapsley* was very pleasant, though we traveled very slowly (10 miles per hour). The current was very strong against us, but the little steamer did its very best. Often we were compelled to stop and "steam up." There were many sandbanks and dangerous rocks, but we had one of the bravest captains on the Congo and he did all in his power to make the voyage a pleasant one for us. We reached our destination in perfect safety and happiness.[28]

In January 1902 Captain Vass took Miss Maria Fearing and all of the girls in the mission's boarding school on an overnight excursion down the Lulua River and back, an experience that none of them ever forgot!

The Capsizing of the First *Lapsley*

For two and a half years the first *Lapsley* was of inestimable value to the American Presbyterian Congo Mission. Both the growing body of African believers and the entire mission staff benefited from the dedicated steamer's faithful service. Each passage made downriver and up was a miracle of God's providential care, for the danger-fraught waters of the monstrous river constantly threatened the fragile vessel.[29]

The first few days of the final journey were accurately described by the Reverend Motte Martin, one of the two new missionaries who were on board:

> We left Leopoldville early on the morning of November 11, in as good condition—as Mr. Vass remarked—as he could make her: freshly painted, with improved helm and smokestack and well equipped cabins, the *Lapsley* appeared indeed a handsome boat. But while Mr. Vass pointed out her many good points, he warned us that she was better suited for American rivers then for the Congo with its gigantic caldrons and whirlpools and cross-currents. You must know that the Congo has an outflow second only to the Amazon, but unlike the Amazon, it is confined to a narrow, rocky channel.
>
> His warning soon began to receive only too ample confirmation, for on the second day out, when we reached our first caldron, the steamer was whirled around like a chip, though the helm was hard over. Indeed, it was only the Captain's quickness of thought and action that saved us again and again. At six different places, during those four days, we were thus whirled, at one place even going around twice.

We were forced to encounter these pools, for attempting the middle of the river, where the whirl was least, we not only made no progress, but were driven backwards, so great was the force of the current![30]

Dr. William M. Morrison wrote very frankly to the home church about the inadequacies of the first mission steamer:

The truth might just as well now be admitted that the old steamer was an unsafe boat from the beginning. Mr. Vass and other skilled engineers who examined her pronounced her so. She was 72 feet long and only 12 feet beam; being a flat-bottomed boat, this made her entirely too long for her width. These proportions might have done in a lake or compara-tively smooth water, but not in a stream like the Congo, or most other rivers in the world for that matter, where there are cross-currents and often waves of considerable height. There are some of us who have ridden on the *Lapsley* and have seen how ugly she always behaved in these cross-currents and we were afraid that some day such a disaster would come. . . . Doubtless, no one is to blame for this situa-tion of affairs; it was pardonable ignorance, but ignorance it certainly was, and we profit by the experience.[31]

Captain Vass's account of the capsizing graphically describes the terrifying experience. The steamer had arrived Saturday evening at Kwamouth, the junction of the Congo and Kasai Rivers. Sunday, as was always the practice on the *Lapsley*, was spent quietly with the stern-wheeler tied securely to the bank. Worship services were always held on board, both in Tshiluba, the Bantu language of most of the crew, and in English, for the "foreigners" aboard. It was a welcome time of spiritual refreshment and physical renewal which prepared all aboard for whatever was to come. Captain Vass related the events of the following day:

Monday morning we were off, but had gone only half an hour when we came to a point with a strong current, though not so strong as the current around Ganchus Point, a little below and on the French side. I eased off from shore to strike

The damaged Lapsley *following capsizing at Kwamouth. Courtesy—Department of History, PCUSA, Montreat, North Carolina.*

the current gradually. As we neared it, I put the helm over to bring her up more, but she was very shyish [sic] and would not come up. When I saw this, we were just about to enter the current. I shut off the engines; she careened and I reversed the engines to draw her back and right her up. This has always worked heretofore in similar circumstances, when I could see the current was going to turn us around. At this instant the water whirled up over the deck, the back current wheeled her stern around and I saw that all was up with her. In a few seconds she was bottom upwards and everyone splashing around for life. I found myself among a mass of workmen who began to grab for me as they were snatching at anything in reach. I then swam as quickly as possible away from the steamer and waited, then swam around to the other side and tried to climb up on it. Some of the drowning people from below seized my foot and I think someone must have gotten hold of my coat. This, together with the current, began pulling me under. I called to Zappo who had climbed up onto the steamer. He seized me by the hand when I was almost out of sight. Fortunately, the canoe (a canoe is always towed alongside), which was full of wood, was not upset. The steamer came up underneath it, so it was resting on the steamer, as it floated, bottom side up. Quickly I had the wood thrown out and sent men to pick up Martin, who was clinging to a wicker chair he had bought in the Madiera Islands. Slaymaker was nowhere in sight; I had last seen him holding to the ship's railing as it went down. I fear he became entangled among a crowd and was carried down by them, or perhaps he was sucked under in attempting to cling to the steamer. He had said he was a good swimmer. Martin, who did not know how to swim, was seized around the neck by one man and they both went down together, but he had a strong grip and succeeded in breaking away. He came up considerably strangled and almost exhausted, just as his wicker chair floated within reach.

The steamer floated along near shore. The people who had crawled up onto it began to wail and cry in the traditional manner. I stopped them all and we knelt and had a short prayer. From then on, no one drowned. As we passed close to the shore the good swimmers dived in and swam out. The canoe then returned with Martin and one or two others who had been picked up. I got the women all in and some of the men and sent them ashore. We were all the while drifting on down stream. I had taken off my shoes, coat, etc., to be ready to swim should she run on rocks and turn again and sink. Once I felt the stack grate over a reef of rocks, but she floated along all right and when the canoe arrived, we all got in and made for shore. The canoe had only one paddle, so the returning was very slow, as we paddled with our hands. I saw the *Lapsley* drift around a point.

We then decided to walk to Kwamouth, about seven or eight miles. That evening Martin had fever; fortunately, I was all right. The next day we came down to Leopoldville on the *Brabant*, a state steamer. The *Lapsley* had in the meantime floated on down and lodged on a grassy point fifteen

kilometers below Kwamouth. The chef de poste sent out
men to search for Slaymaker's body. I also offered a large
reward, but the Great Congo River claims his body—it was
never recovered.[32]

The Reverend Henry Calvin Slaymaker was a native of
Alexandria, Virginia. An ordained elder of the Second Presbyterian Church of that city, he was appointed by the Executive
Committee of Foreign Missions to be the first business manager of
the American Presbyterian Congo Mission, in charge of the trea-
sury and the various accounts. With a warm, affectionate,
outgoing personality, he was much loved by all who knew him,
including his new coworkers whom he had known for only a short
time.

In all, twenty-three of the forty native crew members were
drowned, as well as Mr. Slaymaker, one of the two new missionaries. The January 1904 issue of the *Kasai Herald* listed the names of
all the dead. Women and children had also been aboard, for the
wives of some of the crew had gone along to prepare their daily
meals.

Meanwhile, back at Luebo, the long days of waiting and
wondering continued to pass. At that time, there was no direct
way of communication from Leopoldville into the interior.

Rev. L. A. DeYampert described what happened at Luebo when
news of the tragedy reached the mission:

> It was one bright Sabbath morning late in December, our
> church bell was ringing and the happy congregation was
> gathering into our large shed at Luebo for morning service.
> We had long waited for the return of our steamer *Lapsley*. . . .
> It had long overstayed the time we had expected her. Thus,
> when on that Sabbath morning we heard the shrill sound of a
> steamer whistle away down the river, we could not resist the
> temptation to rush to the beach. The whistle kept blowing
> and soon the crowds that were coming to church turned and
> there was a general rush of all, even those who were in
> church, to the river, to hail the return of what we hoped was
> our own *S. N. Lapsley*.

You can imagine our consternation when, as we neared the river, we were told that our steamer had turned over far down the Congo stream and that "All were dead." A runner came screaming this sad news.

As we reached the river, the steamer was nearing the beach and we looked to see if we could find Mr. Vass or either of the new missionaries we were expecting, Messrs. Martin and Slaymaker. What greater disappointment could we have than to find that only Mr. Martin had come, with just a few of the crew who had gone away on the *Lapsley*!

A steamer of the Kasai Rubber Company brought up the much damaged cargo and the few survivors of our misfortunate steamer. Mr. Vass had remained at the Pool to help arrange for the salvaging of the damaged *Lapsley* and the transport of mission goods for the season. It was a sad hour indeed when the steamer landed and soon there began a wailing of the bereaved relatives that is hard to describe. We went on board and met Mr. Martin, who had been in a most marvelous way saved, and the few surviving crew members who were in a sad dilemma and still grief stricken for their comrades.

That day was turned into one of sorrow and for many long weeks there was a continual wailing in the surrounding villages.[33]

Salvaging the Damaged Steamer

For two weeks the capsized *Lapsley* remained bottom side up where she had lodged against a bank after drifting fifteen kilometers downriver. Captain Vass finally secured help from the state to pull the damaged hulk back into upright position and tow it down to the mission dock at Leopoldville.

Most of the cargo, including a new printing press was salvaged. Rev. Motte Martin regretted the loss of the beautiful foot-pedal organ he had hoped to take to Luebo. The *Lapsley's* hull,

Survivors who helped salvage most of the cargo from the Lapsley. *Courtesy—Department of History, PCUSA, Montreat, North Carolina.*

boiler, and engines were intact; but the upper cabin was gone, the pipes, stanchions, and sundeck a twisted mess, covered with mud and splintered wreckage. Said Martin: "The dear old *Lapsley* looked like a floating junk shop!"

Providentially, the director of the Company Kasai himself passed through Leopoldville just at that time, on his way home to Belgium. He had a partially loaded company steamer going up the Kasai River to Butala in two days and immediately gave permission for this steamer to take all the survivors and a load of cargo. Fortunately, a large load of cargo had been left in the Leopoldville warehouse because the *Lapsley*, on her last journey, had been unable to carry it. This unexpected provision of transportation was free, for commercial steamers were not allowed to carry transport for others *for pay* without special permission from the governor himself. It was this steamer that as a special favor took Mr. Martin, the remaining crew, and the cargo all the way to Luebo.

Captain Vass remained in Leopoldville to overhaul the machinery and the printing press before rust could accumulate and to open the wet cargo, spreading the bolts of trade cloth to dry before they began to rot. He wrote to the home church executives:

> I think it is best to sell the *Lapsley* as she stands, to whomever will take her. I imagine that she could bring $8,000, possibly a little more, as she stands. Then, we should undertake to build a proper steamer for our work, a steamer with sufficient beam and speed to go straight in strong currents, thus avoiding all whirls and whirlpools; there is no danger in a properly constructed boat. In this work I stand ready to do whatever I can. I shall do as you decide, whatever it may be, but am confident that in the long run the rebuilding of the *Lapsley* will not be the cheapest.[34]

Mr. T. Hope Morgan, director of the Congo Balolo Mission, wrote a long letter of sympathy to the Executive Committee of Foreign Missions of the Presbyterian Church in the United States, giving a full account of the disaster and advising:

> The *Lapsley* lies at the beach, a perfect wreck as far as cabins, etc., but the hull is good. Mr. Vass is busy getting the cargo dried and saving all he possibly can. The blow to him is very severe, as all the responsibility of running the boat came upon him. He is one of the few who had charge of boats that I cared to travel with, for he was always most careful in the handling of his boat.
>
> I am sorry to state that your mission will experience great difficulty in getting supplies for your missionaries. All the State boats are heavily laden. Still we will do all we can to get the supplies. If we can render any assistance to you as a mission in whatever course you may decide regarding your boat, please command me.
>
> The steamer is certainly too small for your needs, and does not offer sufficient accommodation for your passengers. It is quite possible, I think, to dispose of her here if you decide to do so. There is one thing you must bear in mind, that it is absolutely needful that you have a boat of your own. A few

years ago you could do without a Mission Boat, but today the Company boats are full and the State boats are all crowded for use of the Katanga Trust and can give no guarantee. You are, therefore, bound to place your own boat on the river.[35]

Memorial

Names of Those Drowned—November 16, 1903
Rev. Henry C. Slaymaker—Born in Alexandria, Virginia, 1873.

Katedi	Kapinga	Kalembi
Kasonga	Kabasele	Kankolonga
Bantonda	Bashishi	Disashi
Ilunga	Fenka	Chersi (Ba-Congo)
Katshetuha	Kasombula	Kazide
Kalua	Kazide	Lubanda
Masenga	Makenshi	Ntamba
Ndi	Child of Ndi	

(*Nearly all were Christians.*)[36]

Notes

1. *Life and Letters of Samuel Norvell Lapsley, Missionary to the Congo Valley, West Africa, 1866–1892* (Richmond, Va.: Whittet and Shepperson, Printers, Tenth and Main Streets, 1893), March 10, 1891, diary entry, 134.
2. Julia Lake Kellersberger, *A Life for the Congo, The Story of Althea Brown Edmiston*, 47–48.
3. Ibid.
4. Ibid.
5. Arthur Rowbotham, "Our Congo Mission" (June 1893): 222
6. "The Congo Boat," *The Missionary* (February 1893): 331–32.
7. Ibid.
8. "A.Good Example," *The Missionary* (March 1893): 114.

9. List of Donors, *The Missionary* (February 1893): 80.

10. "Come Children!" *The Missionary* (July 1893): 270.

11. "The Congo Boat," *The Missionary* (July 1895): 331–32.

12. DeWitt C. Snyder, "A Red-Letter Day at Luebo," *The Missionary* (November 1898): 507.

13. William M. Morrison, "The Late War as Reported on the Congo," (January 1899): 29.

14. Minutes of Executive Committee of Foreign Missions, Presbyterian Church, U.S. (June 6, 1899): 6–8.

15. S. H. Chester, "The Congo Boat; Dear Young Readers," *The Christian Observer* (August 23, 1899): 16.

16. "Dedication of the Congo Boat," *The Richmond Times* (June 24, 1900): 1.

17. "Dedication of the Congo Boat," *The Southwestern Presbyterian* (July 19, 1900): 5–6.

18. "Announcement of the Shipment of the *Samuel N. Lapsley* to the Congo," *The South Western Press* (August 20, 1900).

19. James Boswell, *Journal of a Tour to the Hebrides with Samuel Johnson LL.D.*, now first published from the original manuscript, prepared for the press, with preface and notes by Frederick A. Pottle and Charles H. Bennett (New York: The Viking Press, 1936), 99, 109.

20. Entries in William M. Morrison's diary, March 10, 1899, and March 12, 1899, Archives, Department of History, Presbyterian Church (U.S.A.), Montreat, North Carolina.

21. Mary Dabney, "Bids for Reassembling the *Lapsley*," *Light in Darkness*, 62 and *The Missionary* (March 1904): 110.

22. L. C. Vass, "Arrival of *Lapsley* at Stanley Pool," *The Missionary* (January 1901): 20.

23. L. C. Vass, "Steamer Notes," (Public thanks to state authorities), *The Kasai Herald*, vol. I, no. 2 (July 1, 1901): 23.

24. Ibid. (Trial run of the *Lapsley* to Brazzaville.)

25. Undated letter from L. C. Vass describing first upriver trip.

26. William M. Morrison, "Arrival of the *Lapsley* at Luebo," *The Missionary* (September 1901): 406.

27. L. C. Vass, personal papers, account of near-drowning experience on second *Lapsley* trip given in interview with *The Chattanooga News* (1936).

28. Althea Brown, "Arrival at Luebo," *The Missionary* (February 1903): 500–01.

29. L. C. Vass, "How We Get Our Supplies," *The Kasai Herald*, vol III, no. 2 (April 1, 1903): 17–19.

30. Motte Martin, "Fate of the *Lapsley*," *The Kasai Herald*, vol. IV, no. 1 (January 1, 1904): 4–5.

31. William M. Morrison, "The Old Steamer," *The Kasai Herald*, vol. IV, no. 1, 6.

32. Ibid., "The Disaster," 1–3.

33. L. A. DeYampert, "Our Gains Through Losses on the Congo," *The Missionary Survey* (February 1916): 122–23.

34. L. C. Vass, Letter to S. H. Chester, December 3, 1903, *The Missionary* (February 1904): 58–59.

35. T. Hope Morgan, letter to Executive Committee of Foreign Missions, PCUS, *The Missionary* (February 1904): 61.

36. "Memorial to Those Who Drowned," *The Kasai Herald*, vol. IV, no. 1, (January 1904): 1.

Part III

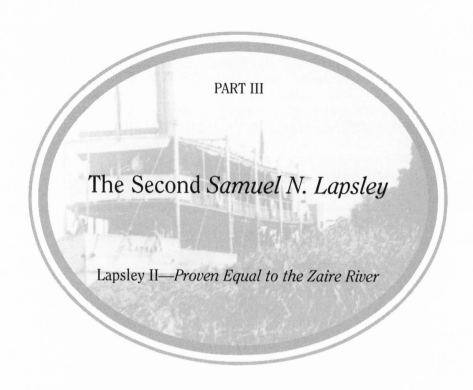

PART III

The Second *Samuel N. Lapsley*

Lapsley II—*Proven Equal to the Zaire River*

The Mission's Plea to the Home Church

WHILE THE AMERICAN PRESBYTERIAN CONGO MISSION had waited ten years for its first mission steamer, now the capsizing of the original *Samuel N. Lapsley* brought a prompt response to an official request for a more adequate replacement. On December 24, 1903, all the missionaries addressed this statement to the Executive Committee of Foreign Missions of the Presbyterian Church in the United States, "humbly advising them to strenuously cooperate in the building of another steamer":

> The *Lapsley*, it is true, has been raised, but her condition is so serious . . ., providing a capable man could be secured . . ., it would take at least a year to repair the steamer, and that, at tremendous expense.

95

We believe that large offers could be secured from the State
and Kasai Company for the [damaged] *Lapsley*. By removing
her upper deck the boat could be used in transporting rubber
on the upper Congo waters. . . . We feel that satisfactory bids
can be secured, and advise acceptance, as this would be the
nucleus of a fund that, with your cooperation, we will soon
have for building a safer and more efficient steamer.

When we speak of the inadvisability of repairing the *Lapsley*,
we only argue for a new steamer. We beg of you not to
consider for a moment the withdrawing of the Mission
steamer, as such action would involve untold inconvenience
and expense. . . . Our cargo would be roughly handled and
damaged, would be irregular in delivery, and we would
have to bear the loss and hardships that would probably
result. We would be in the hands of the uncongenial, and
often unscrupulous trader. . . . All missions, even those of
the steamer-frequented Congo, have given up this method
of transportation for all time, and now own their own
steamers. Indeed, one mission has three steamers, and the
Baptist Missionary Society, with two afloat, is just now
building another large and costly one. If they need it on the
Congo, do we not much more need one on the unfrequented
Kasai? We as a Mission believe we do, and urge that an
adequate boat can be secured now by striking while "the
iron is hot."[1]

Prompt response of the executive committee was:

After carefully considering the matter, we decided it was
our duty to do these things:

First, to call three additional men to be sent out at the earliest
possible day to reinforce the African Mission.

Second, to instruct Mr. Vass to dispose of the present
steamer for the most he can get for it in its present condition.

Third, to call on the Church for funds to build at once a new
and larger steamer.

The alternative to this last proposition, it seems to us, is to abandon the African Mission, a suggestion which we know would be at once and indignantly repudiated by the Church. The present steamer has proven to be not only inadequate for the growing needs of the Mission, but dangerous, on account of its small size and the character of the river. The State, under present conditions, certainly cannot be relied on to do our transport for us. The other missions, as is made evident from Mr. Morgan's letter, cannot do it for us. We must do it ourselves, and in order to do it, we must have a new and larger boat. . . .

The Committee is confident that such a boat as we must have for our work cannot be built and placed on the river for less than $30,000. It is hoped that as much as $5,000 may be realized from the wreckage of the *Lapsley*. We therefore appeal to the Church to give us at once a special contribution of $25,000, in order that we may proceed immediately to building the new boat. This will provide relief for our friends at Luebo, who may be suffering now for necessary supplies, but also for the enlargement of the work of the most wonderfully blessed, as well as most sorely tried, of [all] our [Presbyterian] missions.[2]

At its January meeting, the executive committee "requested Dr. Morrison temporarily to lay aside the work in which he has been engaged in order to raise the necessary funds for building a new *Lapsley*. It was also agreed that his furlough be extended for him to complete the work of publishing his Tshiluba dictionary and grammar."[3]

The February meeting "authorized Mr. Vass, while in England, to secure plans and specifications for building the new boat. After securing them, he is to come at once to America without making any definite arrangement for building."

At this same meeting the bill of the Congo Independent State for raising the steamer, *Lapsley*, and towing it back to Leopoldville was presented to the committee. Because the cost was so exorbitant, the decision was made to communicate with the United States ambassador in Belgium, requesting him to bring this matter to the attention of King Leopold "to secure a fair and proper adjustment with the Congo Independent State."[4]

Contracting for the New *Lapsley*

As instructed by the Executive Committee of Foreign Missions, Mr. Vass returned to the United States after making some inquiries about shipbuilding companies in England.

The special committee appointed for raising the funds for the new mission steamer, Reverend Messrs. Baskette, Chester, Jacobs, Raymond, and Rowland, had been hard at work, aided by special appeals made by Messrs. Stuart and Moffett.[5] Rev. William Sheppard had presented the Presbyterian Church in the United States a freewill offering of cowrie shells from the Church in the Congo Free State, for helping to build the new boat. This amounted to $303.22, a tremendous sum for people of such low income.[6]

On September 15, 1904, the executive committee's special "Boat Committee" reported on definite plans and estimates for the new steamer.[7] An action taken at the October meeting gave Mr. Vass permission to contact shipbuilding firms for their bids.[8] At the November meeting, he submitted the names of thirteen firms to whom plans for the *Lapsley* had been submitted.[9]

Then, at the March executive committee meeting, a bid from the Newport News Ship Building Company in Virginia for $31,000 was rejected, and Mr. Vass requested and was given permission to go to England for personal investigation of the bids received from there.[10]

At the June meeting, the executive committee put a "cap" on the amount available for the *Lapsley,* and Mr. Vass was instructed not to accept a bid for more than $38,367, the amount in hand.[11]

On July 11, 1905, a cable was received by the committee from Mr. Vass asking for permission to accept the bid of Lobnitz & Company, Limited, of Renfrew, contracting to build the new *Lapsley* for five thousand pounds (twenty thousand dollars).[12]

The regular August committee meeting gave the missionary full permission to accept this bid and proceed at once to the constructing of the steamer.[13]

Slowly, carefully, deliberately, all plans for the second *Lapsley* were made "decently and in order." This time, the members of the executive committee were not about to be railroaded into a hasty decision.

Back to Scottish Roots

Following the disaster of the first *Lapsley*, Dr. William M. Morrison had written of Mr. Vass:

> When the *Lapsley* was sent out in many hundreds of separate pieces with no skilled captain or engineer to put her up and launch her at Stanley Pool, Mr. Vass threw himself into the breach. He was possessed of no practical knowledge whatever in such matters—he simply had a remarkable talent for tools, an indomitable will and tireless energy, a resourceful cleverness, and above all an unfaltering faith that God would help him through. When the government and the trading companies were evidently congratulating themselves on the prospect of getting an enormous sum for putting up the boat, they were all greatly chagrined when the intrepid Vass said, "Well, I'll put it up myself." And he did. It took many weeks of hard work under the most trying circumstances, but the task was completed.[14]

Now facing an even larger, more technically complicated job, Mr. Vass was well-equipped by three years of mechanical experience of the most practical kind, plus nautical skills gained in fighting the river itself. Even as he had knelt on the bottom of the capsized steamer, praying with his surviving crew for those they had lost and praising God for their own narrow escape, his mind was busily at work. Already he was formulating the necessary dimensions and power specifications for a vessel that would be the equal to the river.

In 1896, Dr. Lachlan Cumming Vass Sr., had been appointed an official delegate of the Presbyterian Church in the United States to the joint meeting in Glasgow, Scotland, of the Pan-Presbyterian and Evangelical Alliances. Dr. and Mrs. Vass took their two sons with them on this trip of several months' duration. Lachlan Jr.,

Columbia Seminary graduate, was given permission to be absent from his first pastorate. Edward, just graduated from Davidson College, would be entering medical school in the fall. The family visited the ancestral home of James Vass, Dr. Vass's father, who had grown up at Forres, on the Firth of Moray, and also visited relatives in Inverness, stronghold of his grandmother's Cumming clan. Dr. Vass had close ties with his Scottish roots and it was at this time that his son Lachlan Jr. became acquainted with his cousins living in Scotland. Now, the young missionary had a growing inner conviction that nothing could be better suited to the thriving African mission of the Presbyterian Church in the United States, which also had strong, Scottish roots, than a sturdy "Scots" river steamer, born on the Clyde River.

On his way back to the States a few months earlier, Mr. Vass Jr. had carefully observed the work of different shipbuilding companies in England and Scotland. As a result of his own river-navigation experiences, he had some firm convictions as to design. For instance, he did not want an extension of the hull between the wheels that some stern-wheelers had. Neither did he want a shape at the bow like the *Endeavor*, which had no keel. In addition, he wanted only one large, powerful boiler, weighing eleven tons, which would be located *before*, not aft![15]

Twice he visited the Salter docks at Oxford where the Baptist Missionary Society's *Endeavor* was then under construction. However, he decided against this company, for it had never designed a craft for tropical rivers before the *Endeavor* and because

> . . . they cannot guarantee 9 knots. They have absolutely no way of telling whether she can make it at Oxford. There is hardly a mile run there and the water is shallow, which makes it impossible [to test accurately the engines] so that they can approximate the speed.[16]

He could find no shipbuilders who would guarantee an absolute ten-knot speed, with twenty-five tons of dead weight. They all said it was a physical impossibility with a three-foot draft. He was determined to have the new *Lapsley* made where its top speed could be tested on an officially measured mile such as that on the Clyde River.

For many different reasons no company seemed more experienced or better qualified to construct the second *Lapsley* than Lobnitz & Company, Limited, of Renfrew, Scotland. So, this was the one he unreservedly recommended to the home Church.

Plans and Specifications

In August 1905, Lachlan Vass wrote this letter which was later published in the denomination's official organ, *The Missionary*:

> We are now glad to announce that a contract has been signed with Messrs. Lobnitz & Co., Limited, shipbuilders, Renfrew, Scotland, for the new boat.
>
> Renfrew is one of the many small shipbuilding towns on the Clyde, only a few miles below Glasgow. The firm which is to build our steamer has had large experience in building stern-wheel steamers for tropical rivers, having supplied a number for the Congo, and others for the Amazon, Niger and rivers of India. The *Lapsley* is to be built and erected complete, tried for speed and stability on the Clyde under various conditions to our entire satisfaction, then taken apart and delivered, ready for shipment by steamer and rail, to Leopoldville, on the Congo. The contract price for the work complete is $24,250.
>
> The firm expects to have the work finished about December, so we may be able to take out the new steamer as a Christmas present to the faithful workers and expectant Christians at Luebo and Ibanj [sp], who have been, as they say, "listening for many moons for the sound of the *Lapsley's* whistle."
>
> The new boat will be greatly superior in every way to the old one. She will have a ninety-foot hull, one hundred and five feet over all, and a nineteen-foot beam, and with a speed on trial, with cargo, of not less than nine knots. There will be two working decks. On the upper will be placed four sleeping cabins, bath room and dining salon. . . .

All of the upper cabins are provided with double roofs to protect the occupants from the fierce heat of the tropical sun. In front of the salon is a large deck space where Sunday services will be held when we are away from Luebo.

On the lower or main deck are the boiler and engines, also the galley, two pantries for barter goods and provisions, a tool house, a small cabin for the head native engineer, and a workbench. On this deck will be the large crew necessary for cutting wood in the forests every night.

We believe that we can safely predict that there will not be a better, more serviceable or comfortable mission steamer among the eight or ten now on the Congo. The committee has taken every precaution to make the steamer a success, and have secured the best expert help in checking and revising all plans, that no mistakes might occur. The work will be under the constant inspection of a skilled naval architect and consulting engineer who is independent of the firm doing the work. . . .

We feel sure that it has been best to come here, and are confident that no better place than old Presbyterian Scotland could have been chosen in which to build the *Samuel N. Lapsley*, with which to send the sound Calvinistic doctrine of grace and love to the heart of Central Africa.[17]

The more technical aspects of steamship construction that so occupied Mr. Vass's mind at that time are evident in a personal letter to Mr. Morgan:

Our boat is constructed on an entirely different principal from the *Endeavor*, the Baptist Missionary Society steamer. I suppose they will, of course, say theirs is by far the best. I don't blame them! I would do the same if I were in their place! It is this way: Their boat is, I believe, planned to be on an even keel when lying light. This means that they had to cut away, or slope up the bottom at the bow, so that when loading, theoretically, they can distribute their cargo evenly. This, of course, lowers the wheel that much deeper into the water. With feathering paddles, it will not be so bad as with radial wheel boats; but, when fully loaded, they still have the strain of the extra weight of boiler and machinery at each end. Thus, there is the usual amount of strain and tendency to buckle. This, I suppose, is all well taken up by bracing . . . though I prefer the bracing we have adopted.

Now, our boat is on this principal: The submersion of the wheel remains the same, whatever the cargo up to about 20 tons. When light, she will not be on even keel, but her head will rise more than the stern. In short, she is to have a pivotal point at or near the shaft of the wheel. If you notice, she is a great deal deeper at the stern than the *Livingstone* and thus should not settle at the stern, necessitating weighting at the bow to lift the wheel to a proper place for running. The *Endeavor* will have a greater carrying capacity, I expect, as she is lighter, with buffer lines, and I think our engines will be a little heavier. I have purposely built her with less cabin room and more deck space.

Well, we will have to wait and see who has the best boat! There is this to say, however; they say in print that the *Endeavor* is costing about 5,800 pounds. Well, the *Lapsley* is costing only 5,000 pounds! The *Endeavor* was the first stern-wheeler Salter had ever built, while Lobnitz has built them by the dozens for various tropical rivers. I hope they will both be a success and greatly advance the Lord's work on the Congo and Kasai Rivers.[18]

The *Lapsley's* Birthplace

As the second *Lapsley* began to take shape under a large shed on the banks of the Clyde, her diminutive size and distinctive shape became increasingly apparent, in comparison to the ocean giants under construction around her. Directly across the river two large merchant ships were taking shape. A little distance below them, a twenty-thousand-ton Cunard liner for the New York-Liverpool service was being built. Also, subsidized by the British government in the same yards, was a twenty-five-thousand-ton liner being built which would travel at a speed of twenty-six knots. Just above the *Lapsley's* dock were two huge Canadian Pacific steamers nearing completion and a large battleship with other war vessels visible in the distance.

Mr. Vass explained an interesting fact about the Clyde River:

> From Glasgow to where the Clyde empties into the Firth of Clyde its banks are thickly dotted with great ship-building yards. For most of this distance the river is so narrow that the great ocean vessels all have to be built pointing down stream. When they are launched, great cables or chains with huge anchors attached are fastened to them so that the momentum of the ship will be quickly slackened when they enter the water. Otherwise, even at this angle, they would crash into the opposite bank.[19]

According to the Lobnitz & Company's Contract Number 609, the net price for the steamer complete was five thousand pounds sterling, payable in cash in four installments, as follows:

> 10 percent on signing contract
> 30 percent when hull is framed
> 30 percent when satisfactorily launched
> 30 percent after satisfactory trial, taken to pieces and packed, delivered free on rail at Renfrew.[20]

On October 16, 1905, Captain Vass joyfully wrote to the home Church:

> We have at last reached the point where we can stand on the real and material deck of the new *Lapsley*. . . . The firm has given notice that the boat is now "in frame," which, according to the contract, means that it is time for making a second payment, which has now been duly paid. . . . Our own *Lapsley* is being brought into existence amidst such congenial surroundings, and we hope during the next month to see her glide from the stocks of Messrs. Lobnitz & Company into the Clyde. On its friendly waters she will make her first trials of

strength and stability. We trust that these will prove sufficient
to do battle successfully with the far greater and much more
dangerous waters of the Congo and the Kasai.

All the time he was in Renfrew, spending every day at the
Lapsley's dock, watching every detailed mechanical procedure of
the construction, Mr. Vass was also watching for the right
machinist among the shipyard workmen to take with him back to
the Congo to assist with the reassembling.

On October 19, 1905, he wrote to Hawkins, his colleague at Luebo:

> I am trying to get a man to go out and help me in the recon-
> struction and work in running the *Lapsley*, and now have a
> man in sight. He is a Scotchman, a machinist by profession,
> and a Baptist in denomination, but I don't think that will
> injure our Presbyterian crowd! He is not a rampant immer-
> sionist and, if necessary, I expect will join the Presbyterian
> church. I am going to write to the Committee this week and
> recommend his appointment to this work. Dr. Chester has
> told me to try and get such a man.

> The Congo railway will not give us any reduction on the
> transport of our boat so we will have to pay in full. The
> Director told me when I was in Brussels that if we asked for
> a donation or gift, they might grant us something as such. I
> reported this to the Committee, but personally advised that
> we should accept no favors from them. Rather than that, we
> should pay in full, as the Church is able to do so, even
> though they are hard pushed financially at Nashville.[21]

Problems and Criticisms

Early in November 1905, Captain Vass received the bid for the
reconstruction of the *Lapsley* from Captain Vita of the Compagnie
Industrielle de Transit au Stanley Pool (CITAS) engineering firm in
Leopoldville. The bid was for the sum of four thousand Belgian
francs. In addition, the mission would have to furnish a paid,
skilled engineer.

Vass promptly wrote to Morgan, the mission's business manager in Leopoldville:

> Tell Captain Vita to go and soak his head or talk sense. . . .
> The CITAS bid will cost us $2,000 just for the reconstruction
> of the boat. I am confident that I can do it myself just as well
> in very little more time and not exceed $1,000! So, you can
> inform him that we have about decided to do it ourselves![22]

Much advice was given and many criticisms were offered by some who had been responsible for the construction of other mission steamers. They said that Vass had made a grave mistake in installing one large boiler rather than two small ones. All the other steamers had two. Also, the *Lapsley* was "too large" and far too heavy and did not have enough cabin accommodations. There was too much deck space. Furthermore, the plans for the new stern-wheeler did not reveal the Lobnitz & Company's patents, which they had hoped to see. To all these criticisms, Mr. Vass simply replied: "Just you wait and see! The Lord is building our boat. I have never taken a step without first praying about it, and so I know the *Lapsley* is going to be a good boat and a success!"[23]

Launching and Dedication of the Second *Lapsley*

On November 29, 1905, the *Samuel N. Lapsley* was successfully launched. One week later the new river steamer underwent her official trials on the Clyde.

Captain Vass wrote exultantly to Dr. Morrison on December 26, 1905:

> Well, it all went off satisfactorily and I believe we have a good
> boat! On the measured mile, she made 9-knots and she does
> not go beyond the 37 inch [limit] with 20 tons of dead weight
> on board. Mr. Steel of the Congo Balolo Mission, who has run
> the *Livingstone* for three years, was aboard and is very much

The second Samuel N. Lapsley, *leaving the shipbuilder's dock on its inaugural run on the River Clyde, Renfrew, Scotland, on December 16, 1905. Courtesy— Department of History, PCUSA, Montreat, North Carolina.*

pleased with her. He says we have a much better boat than the *Livingstone* and he is ready to swap with us any day![24]

December 16, 1905, was a beautiful, clear, and sunny day in Renfrew, Scotland. Such days are extremely rare at that time of year. A gracious Providence was blessing the dedication of the special little stern-wheeler constructed for his service in Central Africa.

Invitations were sent to Church leaders all over the British Isles, especially to those whose churches had missions in Central Africa:

You are cordially invited to be present at the Dedication of the American Presbyterian Congo Mission's steamer at Renfrew, Scotland.

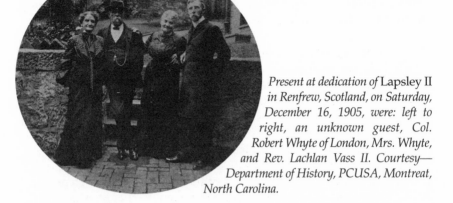

Present at dedication of Lapsley II *in Renfrew, Scotland, on Saturday, December 16, 1905, were: left to right, an unknown guest, Col. Robert Whyte of London, Mrs. Whyte, and Rev. Lachlan Vass II. Courtesy— Department of History, PCUSA, Montreat, North Carolina.*

The Dedication of the Congo Mission steamer, *Samuel N. Lapsley*, will take place at the yards of Messrs. Lobnitz and Company, Limited, Renfrew, Scotland, on Saturday, December 16, 1905.

The Chair will be taken at 11 a.m. by Robert Whyte, Esquire, of London, supported by Messrs. Wilkes, Steel and Vass, missionaries from the Congo.

Rev. George Anderson of the Renfrew Parish Church will offer the dedicatory prayer.

It is hoped that you and your friends may be present.[25]

Some seventy-five people attended the dedication ceremony. All posed on the dock for a picture of those present for a momentous occasion.

Preparations for Shipment to Africa

Captain Vass wrote to Hawkins at Luebo informing him that the Lobnitz workers were now cutting the *Lapsley* down for shipment, so, *she is finished*! He also requested his colleague to begin recruiting woodcutters, who were to be sent downriver to help with the reconstruction of the new mission steamer. There was also a special piece of equipment that Mr. Vass had used in assembling the first *Lapsley*, which he needed to be sent to him:

> When you get this I want you to do the following for me. Go to the steamer store and get my riveting forge, for heating the rivets and send it down to Leo to me. I will need it in the reconstruction of the steamer. Take off the wheel and the part that might be easily broken and see that they are securely fastened to the forge so as not to be lost. Then, look in that cupboard and you will find some small rubber rollers or rings to put on the spindle of the fan of the forge bearing against the wheel. Send 2 or 3 of them, also. Send the forge down as soon as possible as I will be out by that time, and notify Morgan that you are sending it so that he can send over to Kinshasa and get it.[26]

To Dr. Morrison at Luebo, Vass wrote with satisfaction of the acceptance of William Scott by the Executive Committee of Foreign Missions. After completing the special task of assembling the *Lapsley*, he would be appointed a full missionary, if the mission were in accord.

It took nine long, tedious months for the second *Lapsley* to be designed, constructed, launched, tested, outfitted, and then taken apart and crated for shipment to Matadi, a port in the Congo Free State. On the eve of his departure, Captain Vass wrote: "I will be glad to get away from here. The sun rises about 9 A.M. and sets about 3:30 P.M., then just skirts the horizon behind clouds and is seldom seen. It is always night here."[27]

———•———

Twenty-seven years of faithful service were given to the American Presbyterian Congo Mission by this dependable stern-wheeler, so carefully constructed in Scotland. After being sold in 1932 to a commercial company, she continued to ply the waters of the great Zaire River system, the same strong, dependable vessel that she had always been. A Belgian riverboat captain remarked about her to Captain Vass's son, "When your Mission's steamer went up for sale, I did my best to buy her, because she is the finest stern-wheeler on the whole river system. No other steamer comes near her in power and design." Amazingly, the river career of the second *Samuel N. Lapsley* lasted for almost seventy years.

Such was the sturdy river steamer, dedicated to fruitful, faithful service on that cold December day in 1905!

Plaque on second *Lapsley*:

NO. 609
LOBNITZ & CO. LTD.
ENGINEERS & SHIPBUILDERS
RENFREW.

Sequel to the Saga

Working in the old Luebo station storeroom one day in 1967, American Presbyterian Congo Missionary Reverend Howard D. Cameron found the brass plaque from the *Lapsley* bearing the above inscription. Mr. Cameron wrote to Lobnitz & Company in Renfrew, Scotland, and received the following reply:

> No. 609 was the Yard Number for a Stern Wheel Steamer built by Lobnitz & Co. Ltd., Renfrew, for the Executive Committee of Foreign Missions of the Presbyterian Church in the United States (Incorporated), Nashville, Tenn. The contract was dated 1st August 1905 and the contract sum was 5,000 pounds Sterling. The vessel measured 105 ft. x 19 ft. x 4'9" and was probably a little beauty in its day. Doubtless also it did excellent work in transporting the missionaries from station to station and may well give you quite a nostalgia in retrospect. I doubt if I can usefully add

anything else as our records since moving from Renfrew are rather scant. If however you have any particular query, please don't hesitate to drop me a line.

J. L. Ferguson [signed]
SIMONS-LOBNITZ, LTD.
Linthouse, Glasgow, S.W. 1
Scotland

Arrival of the Shipment at Kinshasa

Lachlan C. Vass and William B. Scott left London for Southampton at 9:20 A.M. on February 2, 1906. Embarkation was at 4 P.M. on the Belgian steamer, *Philippeville*, out of Antwerp, bound for the ports of Banana, Boma, and Matadi on the Zaire River estuary in the Congo Free State. The crated *Lapsley* had been shipped to Antwerp for loading onto this steamer.

Six days out to sea, nearing Teneriffe in the Canary Islands, where mail would be left to go back to Europe, Mr. Vass wrote to his mother:

> The *Lapsley* is all safe aboard this steamer, which is quite heavily laden. I have not seen any of our crates, as they are stored away below. You remember that I wrote you that for a while we were missing 31 packages, but they all turned up, so I think our shipment is complete.[28]

The entire *Lapsley* cargo weighed close to one hundred tons. On the narrow-gauge railroad bypassing the lower Zaire cataracts, it filled fourteen flatcars. Not only did it include all the parts of the entire steamer, it also contained the equipment necessary for the task of reassembling one smoothly operating stern-wheeler. There were boxes of regular hammers and "holding-up hammers" for working upside-down inside the hold. All the regular tools, irons, saws, chisels, drills, jacks for lifting, tackling and crowbars for handling the heavy pieces had also been purchased. Of most importance of the supplies was a rough carriage of heavy timbers on small, wide, flanged wheels, on which the eleven-ton boiler would be moved from the railhead to the slipway on the riverbank

Narrow-gauge train which went around the cataracts of the Congo River, Matadi to Kinshasa. Courtesy—Department of History, PCUSA, Montreat, North Carolina.

The crated Lapsley being unloaded from the railroad cars near the Stanley Pool beach. Courtesy—Department of History, PCUSA, Montreat, North Carolina.

and onto the steamer. This was the kind of equipment used in the United States for moving houses.[29]

The initial impressions of a new missionary, observing Africa and Africans for the first time, are always revealing. William Scott's account of the first steps in reassembling the *Lapsley* has just such refreshing insights, noted by a newcomer:

> The *Lapsley*, like the *Lusitania*, was built on the Clyde, Scotland, but she had an experience which the latter did not share, that of being taken to pieces after her trial trip. She was then sent to Glasgow by rail and then shipped to Antwerp, where she was transshipped to Matadi, near the mouth of the Congo River. From Matadi she was sent by rail to Leopoldville where she was [to be] rebuilt. Perhaps some would like to know how the railway folk at Leopoldville handle cargo. Well, the best answer I can give is that they don't handle it at all. When the train comes in, the station-master sends word to the receiver to come and get his goods. There is no provision made for unloading, in fact, it seems as if everything is done more to hinder than to help!
>
> Using a small hand-drawn wagon with a ton's capacity, some old rails and our crowbars, we, with our inexperienced work crew, set ourselves to the task of getting the steamer parts from the railway to the beach, a distance of one-third of a mile. The most difficult part to handle was the boiler which weighs eleven tons without the fittings. The railway gave us from 9 o'clock in the morning till dark to get it off the car and clear the track. This was no easy task, as the boiler is top-heavy, and the ground is soft sand which gives way under a few tons of pressure. It was one of the most tropical days we have experienced since coming to Africa. The [metal] objects got so hot we could scarcely touch them. Then, to add to our discomfort, a thunder-storm came up suddenly, and we were wet and chilled through. Darkness forced us to stop for the day. Next morning we were up before day and had the track clear by seven o'clock.[30]

Reassembling of the New Stern-wheeler

How grateful Lachlan Vass now was for the skilled assistance of W. B. Scott! Without the experienced technology of the professional machinist, selected from among many Clyde River shipyard employees, Captain Vass knew he could never accomplish the formidable task that lay ahead. Officials of the British, Belgian, and Dutch commercial companies with large, power-equipped docking machinery at Stanley Pool watched first with amusement and then amazement as the beautiful little steamer began to take shape. Their attitude might be said to have resembled that of the giant Goliath as he watched the approach of the shepherd lad, David, armed only with his slingshot. Vass and Scott both knew that the rebuilding of the new *Lapsley* would be accomplished only by careful, planned maneuvering combined with brute force, sheer manpower alone!

Vass had already hired a picked crew of native workers, several of whom had helped assemble the first *Lapsley*. With a sharp pang, he could not help but remember the twenty-three faithful souls lost in that tragic capsizing. Most of all, he missed Kiazi, the first ship's cook and evangelist who called the crew together both morning and evening for a brief service of Bible study and prayer.[31]

It was Kankenze whom Mr. Vass most gladly welcomed back to join the ship's crew. The son of Chief Zappo Zap himself, Kankenze was one of those who moved to Luebo with Samuel Lapsley in 1891, on his return trip from Malange (Luluabourg). His natural leadership qualities were soon apparent; he had immediately become an accepted member of the founding missionary's household.

When Lapsley was forced to return to Boma, the Congo Free State capital, in order to legalize the American Presbyterian Congo Mission's ownership of the Luebo station concession, he took Kankenze along with him. Throughout the brief final illness at Matadi, Kankenze cared for his missionary, anticipating every need. He witnessed the quiet, triumphant death and dutifully shepherded the Mukete lad, Shamba Mwana, back to his father at Bena Kasenga, as Lapsley had requested him to do.

Engineer William B. Scott and Captain Lachlan C. Vass II, in Kinshasa, reassembling the second Lapsley. *Courtesy—Department of History, PCUSA, Montreat, North Carolina.*

This capable, highly intelligent young man had helped Vass assemble the first *Lapsley*; he had been the "kapita" or "boss" of the work crew. He was one of the strong swimmers who escaped when that steamer capsized. He had helped pull the captain up onto the bottom of the overturned boat and knelt there with him in prayer. Now, he had made the long journey downriver from Luebo to help put the new steamer together. How good it was to have such a proven and experienced man to serve once again as "kapita" of the new crew![32]

W. B. Scott commented on the adjustment he had to make to working with an all-African team:

> I may say that it was a great change for me, being used to modern workshop life where every man knows his work and everything is in a hurry, to work with a people where

nobody knows [what to do], and where everything goes as slowly as possible. Still we were thankful for each day's progress and I soon felt at home with the people. Sometimes I was surprised at the work they did, and at other times I was just as surprised at what they did not do, as things have a strange way of coming to a standstill when the workmen are left alone.[33]

The personal diary which Mr. Vass kept at this time at Kinshasa gives a concise, simple record of the process and order of assemblage:

Mar. 6, 1906—1st cargo from steamer arrived.

Mar. 8, 1906—Boiler arrived.

Mar. 9, 1906—Began unloading 11-ton boiler—hard work— I collapsed for a short time—did not finish.

The eleven-ton boiler, unloaded, without benefit of power equipment and cranes, from the railroad car, being rolled on logs to the beach. Courtesy—Department of History, PCUSA, Montreat, North Carolina.

Mar. 10, 1906—Got up before daylight; finished unloading boiler by 7 a.m. "as must have line cleared by then."

Mar. 21, 1906—Laid down the first plate of the *Lapsley.*

Mar. 22, 1906—Received last RR wagon load of the steamer. It has been a very hard and tedious job unloading.

Apr. 23, 1906—*Lapsley* well under way. Shell plating completed and now working on deck. Began riveting the hull today.

To his friend, Millard, Vass described the riveting process:

The workmen doing the riveting have to be constantly watched, to see that they do not neglect to properly rivet down every rivet of the thousands they have to heat and drive up. Lying on their backs under the bottom of the boat, it is no easy work and it is a great temptation for them to leave

Riveting the deck plates to the second Lapsley's *hull. Two small forges on the deck heated the rivets red-hot. Heads of those who worked inside the hull are visible. Courtesy—Department of History, PCUSA, Montreat, North Carolina.*

Superstructure being mounted on the hull, in preparation for launching. Courtesy—
Department of History, PCUSA, Montreat, North Carolina.

alone a rivet that has gotten too cool, and pass on to the next
one. If several like this are put in, you have a leaky boat![34]

May 3, 1906—2 coast men arrived from Accra.

May 12, 1906—20 crew members arrived from Luebo. Paid
off one coast man (Naught).

June 6, 1906—Put on last deck plate today. Decks about half
riveted.

June 11, 1906—Started moving 11–ton boiler to beach.

June 18, 1906—Finished taking boiler down to the beach
without a hitch or any accident. Six days of hard work.

June 30, 1906—Began caulking deck today.

July 13, 1906—Filling in earth for building out slip.

The eleven-ton boiler safely mounted on the Lapsley's *hull at riverbank. Courtesy—Department of History, PCUSA, Montreat, North Carolina.*

July 19, 1906—Lower cabin about finished. Finished caulking the half of upper deck which is down.

July 21, 1906—Slip about finished.

July 24, 1906—Putting steam dome on boiler.

Aug. 1, 1906—Began carrying some of the heavier steamer stuff to beach, crankshaft, etc.

Aug. 6, 1906—Have finished getting up all of the railing possible on *Lapsley.*

Aug. 7, 1906—Painting up *Lapsley* hull.

Aug. 8, 1906—Began greasing slip today for launching. We need 10" to 1 foot of water yet. River only rose 1/2" today.

Aug. 12, 1906—Launched today.[35]

The Baptist Missionary Society's *Endeavor* was launched just at the time that Vass and Scott were struggling to move the *Lapsley's* one heavy boiler into place. Mr. Vass noted: "They have riveted up very rapidly; all their rivets were put in *cold*, which I do not like!"[36]

Quite candidly and with evident pride, he wrote to Dr. Morrison, commenting on the *Endeavor*:

> I believe we have a better one than the new Baptist Missionary Society boat, the *Endeavor*. They were greatly humbled last week (because of their very great amount of bragging) when, on their first trial trip, their engine had a rather serious breakdown, a connecting link parting. It was the part that Scott and I both said would be very likely to break. We also told them that we prophesy that their cross-heads will be the next to go. Their foundations to the wheel have proved too light and they are now busy building more on to it to make it stiffer. . . . I told Williams, who was super-intending the work, when I saw the steamer in Oxford, where

Captain Vass and Engineer Scott standing on the upper deck of the Lapsley, *as reassembling nears completion. Courtesy—Department of History, PCUSA, Montreat, North Carolina.*

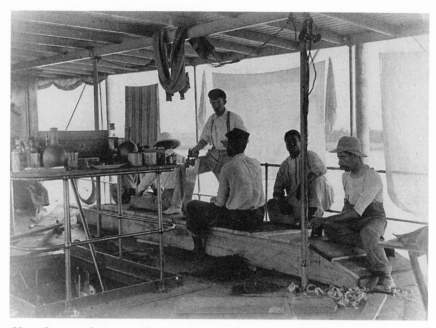

Vass, Scott, and crew members work on making a small skiff for the Lapsley's *use. Courtesy—Department of History, PCUSA, Montreat, North Carolina.*

she was built, that this part of her was far too light. I am sure they have built too light; we are much heavier and stronger in hull and engines, for which they have severely criticized us.

Also, their boat is very ugly and ours will be about the prettiest-looking boat on the river! Howell himself admits that there is not another sternwheeler on the river with as pretty lines. He also admits now that in some parts they *are* too light. Scott sends kindest regards and says he is happy in the work.[37]

And so, with a God-motivated combination of physical prowess, gallons of sweat, clever mechanical strategy and ingenuity, the second *Samuel N. Lapsley* again became a powerful, functioning stern-wheeler. Amazingly, even with moving such a mass of heavy machinery and equipment, there were no accidents, with the one exception of one man whose thumb was broken.

Wrote Scott exultantly: "We are thankful to God for His goodness to us in the work He has given us to do. The *Lapsley* will surely prove herself worthy of the name of a Clyde-built steamer!"[38]

The First Voyage of the New *Lapsley*

The initial voyage in 1906 of the second *Lapsley* upriver to Luebo station was highly significant in mission steamer navigational history. It was also memorable because of the presence on board of seven workers, four of them new recruits. In addition to Captain Vass and Engineer W. B. Scott, there was Dr. William M. Morrison, so gifted in leadership training and linguistics as well as in Bible translation, who had already spent ten years on the field. With him was his bride, Bertha Stebbins Morrison of Gayden, Louisiana. Superb judges of character, the Luebo Christians promptly gave this lovely, radiant lady the fitting Tshiluba name of *Mutoto,* "Star." Two young African Americans from Alabama, the Reverend Adolphus A. Rochester and Miss Annie Kate Taylor, who had met for the first time on this voyage, would later be joined in marriage.

Dr. Llewellyn J. Coppedge, the mission's very first full-fledged physician, was also among the eagerly awaited new personnel on that historic journey. For twelve years Dr. Coppedge directed the first real medical work of the American Presbyterian Congo Mission. When his wife's illness forced the couple to leave Africa, they transferred their medical mission work to Mexico, where they served from 1920–1948.

Mrs. Annie Taylor Rochester recorded in her diary a vivid account of the first journey of the new *Lapsley*:

> Anchored by the bank of the river, at the edge of a dense forest, the *Lapsley* is a beautiful steamer. . . . We could only feel proud of her and be grateful to God that the Mission is to have such splendid provision for communication between Leopoldville and our Mission Station nearly nine hundred miles away. . . .

Captain Vass standing beside the water-injector and boiler. The stern-wheeler was 90 feet in the hull, 105 feet overall, with a 19-foot beam and a cruising speed of nine knots per hour. Courtesy—Department of History, PCUSA, Montreat, North Carolina.

The morning of our departure from Leopoldville, we were all up early, and looked forward to our journey with some anxiety, but with more hope and happiness. We waited for the mail to arrive from Matadi, that we might get all the letters from the friends at home for the missionaries in the far away stations of Luebo and Ibanj [sp]. Missionaries of other denominations came on board to extend congratulations and assure us of their prayers for a prosperous voyage up the rivers. They brought mangoes, goats, fish and plantains. The rather large party of us had a happy dinner together.

It was a sight worth seeing, to go down on the lower deck and view the conglomeration of woodcutters, their wives, children, bags and baggage, all mixed up together. Native passengers and crew all travel on the lower deck. There are bales and bales of freight. The woodcutters have all sorts of uncanny looking bags and bundles. As a rule, they have no bedding. A few are the happy possessors of blankets and palm frond beds and are considered quite wealthy. All this jolly, jabbering or drowsy crowd stand, sit or lie about among the bags and bundles. Evidently they are a company of varied temperaments. Some find things to laugh and talk about all day; others are grumbling and quarreling much of the time; and there are some who seem to pass all the hours in dreamland.

The days come and go during about three weeks it requires to make the upriver trip from Leopoldville to Luebo. We travel in daytime and anchor at night. It would not be possible to pilot the boat at night and it is also necessary that wood-cutters use this time in renewing the supply of fuel. There are many strange sights along the way. Here and there a hippopotamus, and at rare intervals an elephant may be seen. Sometimes we pass a village, but nearly all of the people have moved away from the shores on account of the oppression to which they have been subjected.

At a few villages, services are held by the missionaries. Along the Congo River are scattered here and there the converts that have come down the river from Luebo and Ibanj [sp]. Regular daily prayer services are held on the

Lapsley in the early morning. We do not travel on the Sabbath; the day is observed as a time for rest and worship.[39]

The Midnight Club

The first upriver journey was not without its share of high-spirited activity and fun. Captain Vass referred to himself as a "staid and kiln-dried missionary," but he proved himself to be anything but that as a member of the mysterious "Midnight Club." The agenda of some of the meetings was interesting:

> This official organization is shrouded in the usual mysteries of all fraternities and clubs. But of its real existence, the officers of the ship and the peaceful passengers became fully conscious soon after entering the Kasai River.

> As usual, the meetings were held at night, the place being the broad deck just in front of the salon. The professed aim of the club was mutual help and the procuring of fish for themselves and friends. For this purpose, long lines were trailed from the stern of the steamer every evening after the day's run. All seemed beautiful, and often the table showed some delightful specimens that made the mouth water.

> Days passed and finally complaints began to arrive at the Captain's headquarters. Here is a sample:

> > Monsieur le Capitaine,
> > There is considerable disturbance aboard ship every night, loud talking and laughing. The cupboards in the salon are often visited and provisions for the mornings' meal are missing, while someone is sucking the eggs.
> > > [Signed] Chief Stewardess
> > > and Indignant Passengers.

A week before the *Lapsley* arrived at Luebo, after a trying day's run, and some work on the machinery, to be ready for an early start the next morning, we sat down to a delightful supper. The steamer was lying at a trading post. The Gentlemen of the Company took supper with us and after this was over, gave an entertainment with their Phonograph. Tired, the Captain, Engineer and Crew retired. At midnight, there was heard a shrill cry, then others of deeper tones and the falling of heavy sticks. All was confusion, but above the din could be heard various and numerous commands, "Pull it in!" "No, stick it with a spear!" "No, get a gun and shoot it!" "No, listen to me, I'll fix it!" And so the Surgeon of the Club runs wildly away, returning with a huge tub.

The Engineer, aroused suddenly from a deep sleep, rushes half-clad onto the deck, thinking the Steamer has torn away from her moorings and that steam must be quickly raised to prevent a serious accident. The passengers rush down from the upper deck, trampling on the sleeping crew of woodchoppers lying all around on the deck. What is it all about? The steamer is seen to be lying quietly at the beach.

See the Doctor of Divinity and the Surgeon lowering the huge tub over the edge of the boat and pushing it down under the water. "Now, come on! Bring him over it! Quick!" "Pull! Lift it up!!" And with a slush, a big splutter and splash, they throw a huge fish on the deck. The Engineer is livid with—not anger, but Righteous Indignation! This is the third or fourth night he has been unable to sleep! There is no fun in this for him. But the next day, as all are admiring a fish of over 45 pounds weight, he was ashamed of even "slight" indignation.

The loss of sleep and heavy work of the Surgeon, President of the Club, in doctoring the trampled crew the next day, with the united protestation of the officers of the steamer and the quietly disposed passengers, seems to have been effectual. After the catching of that fish, the "Midnight Club" appears never to have had another meeting. Quiet now reigned every night on the little ship.[40]

Personages in this "Club" may be identified among the *Lapsley* passengers. The "Chief Stewardess" was Mrs. Morrison; Dr. Coppedge was the "Surgeon" and Dr. Morrison, of course, the "Doctor of Divinity," aided and abetted, no doubt, by the captain himself!

The *Lapsley's* Joyous Welcome to Luebo

Captain Vass, in a letter to his mother, written on December 16, 1906, recounted other events of the first upriver journey:

> Well, we are getting up in the neighborhood of Luebo now, and we hope to get there by the 22nd of the month or at the latest the 24th, so that we can be there for Christmas and give them all a present of the new boat, their cargo from Europe and the party of new and old missionaries. I am sure they will be more than glad to see us!
>
> Today is Sunday and, as usual, we are laying up to spend the Sabbath, at least in part, as it should be spent. But today has been a rather busy one in some respects. Dr. Coppedge, Dr. Morrison and Mr. Rochester went out hunting yesterday afternoon after we stopped. They went across the river in the canoe and killed two hippos, landing the one that Dr. Coppedge killed. Well, there is now meat to satisfy even the crew! I sent over the canoe and it has returned three times, loaded with the meat. I had it all cut up and put in piles and they are now all busily engaged in boiling, smoking and drying it, so that we will not have such a smell on the boat. The people get very little meat out here. They almost go crazy when they see so much, and there is a *pile* of hippo!
>
> We have made a very slow trip up, considering the new boat, but we have been heavily loaded and have not had woodchoppers enough to keep us well in wood.[41]

All went well until the steamer became grounded on a sandbar, almost within sight of Luebo. It took two days of hard work to dislodge and float the boat again. An hour's run brought the *Lapsley* around the river bend, within sight of Luebo beach. Thousands from villages near and far stood on the shore shouting, laughing, exclaiming over the amazing sight of the biggest river vessel they had ever seen, with the faces of their family crew members and the group of missionaries crowded along the railings.

As was their custom, the Christians burst into song, exuberantly singing in Tshiluba one old favorite hymn after another. Hammocks were ready for the long-awaited newcomers in which to be carried to the top of Luebo hill. The entire following day, December 24, was spent in public exercises of welcome and praise to God for the miracle of a strong, sturdy, truly adequate mission steamer and the safe arrival of their beloved "Kuonyi Nshila" (Dr. Morrison) and his bride, and the other new missionaries.[42]

Still another happy event occurred in connection with the *Lapsley's* first upriver trip to Luebo. On January 2, 1907, the American Presbyterian Congo Mission, at its annual mission meeting, took the following action regarding the status of W. B. Scott:

> It was moved and unanimously carried that Mr. W. B. Scott be enrolled as a regular member of the Mission, entitled to the rights of a full member, with the proviso that he teach nothing contradictory to the Standards of the Presbyterian Church in the United States.[43]

The Scottish Baptist was more than happy to be not only a regular member of the *Lapsley* crew, but a *bona fide* missionary as well!

The *Lapsley* Proves Her Worth

Leaving Kinshasa on April 9, 1907, a return trip to Luebo was made in only fifteen running days. Of the seventeen days en route, two were Sundays, on which the *Lapsley* and her crew always worshiped and rested. Captain Vass's pride in his new vessel and a bit of competition with another steamer are evident in a letter written at Luebo to his friend Morgan on May 1, 1907:

> On the old *Lapsley*, the quickest trip ever made was 23 running days, usually it required 25 or 26. The currents in the Kasai River were very strong. At Kwamouth, where the first *Lapsley* capsized, they were the strongest I have ever seen— like a mill-race! We caught up with the *Deliverance* and passed her on the fourth day out. She had had a full day's start on us! The next day, being Sunday, when we did not run, she passed us. We did not catch up with her again, as we were running only 7 or 8 hours a day. We found out at the State wood post where we slept one night, that she had left there before daylight. The Captain had said that he did not want us to catch up with him again! He must have been putting in 12 or 14 hours a day, as compared to our 8 hours. We often had to stop at 2 o'clock at a good wooding spot. Most of the forests down that way are under water at this season, but we found plenty of wood at the State wooding posts.
>
> The steamer has worked splendidly all the way up. We did not push her at all. We never made over 26 revolutions and, most of the time, about 24, and often less. We are also pleased with the wood consumption. It is scarcely a fraction over one fathom per hour. This is careful measurement. I think that is a little more than the *Endeavor* requires.[44]

During the five-month-long dry season layover, when navigation was impossible because of low water, the *Lapsley's* captain and mechanic kept busy constructing a new missionary residence, putting a new thatch roof on the steamer store building and setting up the new printing press.[45]

As the rains began again in September, Luebo missionaries were anxious for their steamer to get under way as soon as possible. Some much-needed barter goods that had been ordered had failed to reach Kinshasa in time for the *Lapsley's* previous trip upriver. As a result, the mission was running extremely short on both barter goods and provisions. Pressure was put on the *Lapsley's* crew to take the first opportunity to leave for the Lower Congo. One of the most difficult downriver trips ever made by the mission steamer, could have been avoided by just a "wee bit" more patience.

Stranded Camp

The Lulua River, on which Luebo is situated, has an average annual rise of twelve to fifteen feet. In September 1907, as the rainy season began, it was a foot lower than it had ever been before. When the water began to rise with the first rains, the decision was made to set out on an urgently needed downriver trip. "And thereby hangs a tale that is much more pleasant to tell about than to experience!" wrote Captain Vass.

For a few miles below Luebo, the Lulua River is rocky and narrow. Then, it broadens out into a wide expanse of sandbanks with narrow channels of water surrounding the sandbanks and islands. Using a pole about twelve feet long, one of the crew members had the all-important task of sounding. Whenever the depth of the water measured dangerously shallow, he called out, "*Nsele, muipi!*" (*Nsele* is the Tshiluba word for "loose sand" and *muipi* means "shallow.") Captain Vass described what happened on this trip, when the ominous cry was first heard:

> Which way must we go? There is not much time to consider, but this is certainly the way, so we go on slowly, hoping every minute that it will get better. In a few minutes, it becomes a certainty that there is not sufficient water. With a grinding sound, the steamer settles quietly but firmly on a sandbank.

> All hands over-board! The headman of the 40 or more woodchoppers is howling with all his might at the men standing in the water, pushing and pulling. He yells even louder at the slow ones to obey the "Overboard!" order. Sometimes he resorts to his leather belt to urge up the very slothful ones.

The anchor is gotten out up stream; four men are at the windlass and all other hands are in the water, pushing. Slowly the bow is pulled around, but suddenly the anchor gives way and back the steamer swings to her original position. Again the anchor is put out and again it gives way. A third attempt proves more successful. Slowly, with the pushing and pulling and the engines working, we succeed in getting off. Thus, after several hours of hard work we are again afloat, but horrible to say!—the deepest water is in such a narrow channel that there is not room enough in which to turn around. Back the *Lapsley* swings onto the opposite sandbank! Another two hours is spent in getting off of that one. Once more we are free, as night is coming on; we tie up at the bank for the night.

The next morning, long sticks are cut and pieces of cloth tacked to the tops as flags. With these, we go out in the canoe and begin sounding and staking off the deepest passage it is possible to find. After a few hours, we return to the steamer, having found and staked off a passage with about five feet of water, but even this is very narrow and winding. This place is finally passed, but a short distance farther on we are again firmly stuck on another bank, requiring the same amount of hard work to get us off.

Proceeding a little further, we arrive at a dangerous place, where great clusters of rocks reach halfway across the river. Most of the water rushes over the rocky side while the sand collects on the opposite. Soon, we hear the dreaded cry, "*Nsele!*" from the sounder. The water is only five feet deep and getting shallower. Engines are reversed, but it is too late. With a hard bump, the steamer strikes a rock, whirls around and settles on a large underwater rock, listing hard to starboard.

The holds are quickly opened, to see if a hole has been knocked in at any place. But the good *Lapsley* has withstood the shock magnificently. It is with difficulty that we finally find, in the forward cargo hold, a very slight dent in one of the strong bilge plates.

All cargo now has to be shifted astern. In a few hours we are again safely floating. We tie up for the night and go out the next morning to sound for the best channel. This is found and staked off, lying close to the rocks, and with only five or six feet of water. One more time on the sandbank and many more times out in the canoe, searching for a passage, we finally pass out of the Lulua River. It has taken us four days to cover the distance usually made in only four hours!

To our sorrow, the Kasai River is also found to be very low. We are soon stuck in a place very difficult to get off. For two and a half days we work before we are free. Again we go out in the canoe to sound for the best passage. It is found, and off we go again. Suddenly, without any warning we strike a hidden snag while in deep water and going at full speed. No harm seems to be done to our steamer, but very shortly we are again stuck on a sandbank.

Working in the tropical sun, with little breeze and a hot boiler nearby competing with the sun in heating things up, at such times even the very best that we can do is not enough.

It took us almost an entire day to get off that last sandbank. After going out in a canoe and sounding ahead for a channel, we decided to go no further until the river rises more. We can assure you that there wasn't any moss left on the bottom of the *Lapsley* and probably very little paint!

We were only two and a half days journey overland to Luebo, so we sent word to them and secured the necessary barter goods for buying food for the crew from the local Bakuba villages. Our place of refuge is on a small island. Our crew quickly built a village of several small grass huts, which we have officially named, "Stranded Camp."

After two weeks, the water began to rise again and once more the faithful *Lapsley* was off on her downriver journey. From "Stranded Camp" on there was very little trouble. True, those on board were stuck on sandbanks two more times, but succeeded in floating the steamer with comparative ease and completed the nine-hundred-mile trip downriver to Kinshasa. At the end of his description of this hazardous journey, Captain Vass wrote: "The *Lapsley* has worked and handled splendidly throughout this very trying trip."[46]

The *Lapsley* Loses Her Builder and First Captain

The last year that the Reverend Lachlan C. Vass Jr. served as captain of the *Lapsley* was 1908. In spite of increasingly frequent bouts of malaria and dysentery, he completed the year's work, making three round trips during the high-water, rainy season months. A justified note of pride was sounded in a letter to his mother, written on April 2, 1908:

> We tied up at 3:30 one afternoon; the State Boat caught up with us about 6 p.m. We easily passed her the next morning. Though this boat left Leopoldville three days before we did, we caught up with her and passed her on the fifth day. That shows what a good runner the *Lapsley* is![47]

On one of Captain Vass's last trips, he sighted from the wheelhouse the body of a dead elephant floating downriver. The good *Lapsley* responded at once to the order to slow down and to a spin of the wheel in the direction of the half-submerged carcass.

A rope thrown from the deck lassoed the protruding head, enabling the crew to pull the animal alongside. One tusk was discovered to have been removed, but the other was still in place on the other side. This remaining almost six-foot-long tusk was found to weigh eighty-five pounds. On examination it revealed a crack running almost its full length, perhaps from a fight with another elephant or by the weight of uprooting a large tree. Amazingly, this fracture had healed itself by forming a large ridge of new growth inside the length of the tusk.

This unique tusk would become the favorite Congo artifact in the Vass's home for many years, always resting on the hearth,

Captain Vass (right) with friends at Boma, before leaving for the United States in 1909. He was the houseguest of British Consul Thesiger (left). (Note crocodile skulls on floor.) Courtesy—Department of History, PCUSA, Montreat, North Carolina.

curved around the living room fireplace. Today it is mounted and housed at the Department of History Museum of the Presbyterian Church (U.S.A.) at Montreat, North Carolina.

Included in the 1908 Annual Report of the American Presbyterian Congo Mission to the executive committee was the statement: "Our steamer, the *Lapsley*, is proving a very satisfactory boat, and we have been well supplied with goods during the past year, for which we thank God!"[48]

In its January 22, 1909, meeting, Mr. Vass was granted permission to resign and instructed to request the Executive Committee of Foreign Missions to secure his replacement for the steamer department of the mission.[49] He sailed from Matadi on March 4, 1909, bringing ten years of faithful, physically demanding labor to a close. In one of his last letters from the field he wrote: "May God continue to bless and protect this steamer, built for and dedicated to His service in Central Africa."[50]

Lachlan Vass's final resignation from the American Presbyterian Congo Mission became official on receipt of the following letter dated July 12, 1910, received at the home of his brother Dr. Edward Vass, in Schenectady, New York:

> Dear Brother Vass,
> I have presented your letter of June 7th, which came too late for last Committee meeting. The Committee accepts your resignation, to take effect on August 31st. In doing so, we desire to express to you our profound appreciation for the service you have rendered the Committee in connection with the two *Lapsleys*, a service which we believe could not have been rendered by any other living man. We shall always hold you in grateful remembrance for your work and labor of love and shall expect you to lend your utmost energies, which we know you will gladly do, in behalf of the great Foreign Mission cause in connection with your work at home.
> With kindest regards and best wishes,
> Fraternally and truly yours,
> S. H. Chester [signed]
> Secretary, Executive Committee of Foreign Missions
> Presbyterian Church in the United States

Notes

1. "Statement of the Congo Mission," *The Missionary* (March 1904): 107–08.

2. "The Committee of Foreign Missions' Appeal for $25,000 for a New *Lapsley*," *The Missionary* (February 1904): 55–56.

3. Minutes of the Executive Committee of Foreign Missions (June 1903–March 1914), entry of January 12, 1904; action regarding William M. Morrison.

4. Ibid., entry of February 1904; action regarding Vass en route to U.S.A., and instructions to investigate shipbuilding companies in Great Britain.

5. Ibid., entry of January 12, 1904; action regarding Committee of Appeal for Funds for the *Lapsley*.

6. Ibid., entry of August 9, 1904; action regarding reception of gifts from native churches at Luebo and Ibanji for a new *Lapsley*; gift delivered by Sheppard.

7. Ibid., entry of September 15, 1904; action regarding plans and estimates for new steamer.

8. Ibid., entry of October 11, 1904; action regarding permission to take bids for the *Lapsley* from shipbuilding firms.

9. Ibid., entry of November 1904; action regarding thirteen firms to which plans were submitted for building bids.

10. Ibid., entry of March 14, 1905; action regarding rejection of Newport News firm's bid and permission to Vass to go to England.

11. Ibid., entry of June 8, 1905; action regarding amount now available.

12. Ibid., entry of July 11, 1905; action regarding Vass cable requesting permission to sign contract with Lobnitz for twenty thousand dollars.

13. Ibid, entry of August 8, 1905; action giving approval for building new *Lapsley*.

14. "Rev. L. C. Vass, Captain of the *Lapsley*," *The Missionary* (March 1904): 110.

15. Personal letter of Vass to Morgan from Renfrew, Scotland, July 29, 1905.

16. Ibid.

17. "The New *Lapsley*—Work Begun," *The Missionary* (September 1905): 438–39.

18. Personal letter of Vass to Morgan, August 9, 1905.

19. "The New *Lapsley's* Birthplace, Building the Steamer on the Clyde," *The Missionary* (December 1905): 78–79.

20. Contract No. 609 with Lobnitz & Company for "Building One Sternwheeler River Steamer," sixth clause on page 2, "Payments."

21. Personal letter of Vass to Hawkins about Scott, October 19, 1905.

22. Personal letter of Vass to Morgan, November 9, 1905.

23. Ibid.

24. Personal letter of Vass to Morrison, November 28, 1905.

25. Invitation to Dedication Ceremony of *Lapsley*, Saturday, December 16, 1905.

26. Personal letter of Vass to Hawkins, November 28, 1905.

27. Personal letter of Vass to Morrison, December 26, 1905.

28. Personal letter of Vass to his mother, February 7, 1906, and personal letter of Vass to Morgan, September 25, 1905.

29. Personal letter from Vass to Rev. J. A. Millard, August 13, 1906.

30. W. B. Scott, "The Rebuilding of the *Lapsley*," *The Kasai Herald* (January 1, 1908): 4–5.

31. "The Lost Among the Native Crew," *The Missionary* (March 1904): 109.

32. J. Hershey Longenecker, "Kankenze, Son of Zappo Zap," *Lumu Lua Bena Kasai* (May 1933): 5.

33. W. B. Scott, "The Rebuilding of the *Lapsley*," *The Kasai Herald* (January 1, 1908): 5.

34. Personal letter from Vass to Rev. J. A. Millard, August 13, 1906.

35. Personal diary of L. C. Vass.

36. Personal letter of Vass to Morgan, March 25, 1906.

37. Personal letter of Vass to Morgan, June 12, 1906.

38. W. B. Scott, "The Rebuilding of the *Lapsley*," *The Kasai Herald* (January 1, 1908): 5.

39. *The Missionary Survey* (June 1912): 625–26.

40. L. C. Vass, "The Rise and Fall of the Midnight Club," *The Kasai Herald*, no. 1 (January 1907): 2–3.

41. L. C. Vass, letter to his mother, December 16, 1906.

42. T. C. Vinson, *William McCutchan Morrison, Twenty Years in Central Africa* (Presbyterian Committee of Publication, Texarkana, Arkansas-Texas, 1921), 71–72.

43. Mission Meeting Minutes of the American Presbyterian Congo Mission, January 2, 1907, 96–97.

44. L. C. Vass, letter to his mother, April 21, 1907.

45. L. C. Vass, letter to Morgan, May 1, 1907.

46. L. C. Vass, personal papers, typed description of "A Trying Trip on the Congo River," written at Leopoldville, Congo Free State, October 23, 1907.

47. L. C. Vass, letter to his mother, April 2, 1908.

48. Annual Letter of the American Presbyterian Congo Mission to the Executive Committee of Foreign Missions of the Presbyterian Church in the United States, printed in the *Kasai Herald* (January 1909): 14.

49. Mission Meeting Minutes of the American Presbyterian Congo Mission, January 22, 1909.

50. L. C. Vass, letter to his mother, April 2, 1908.

Part IV

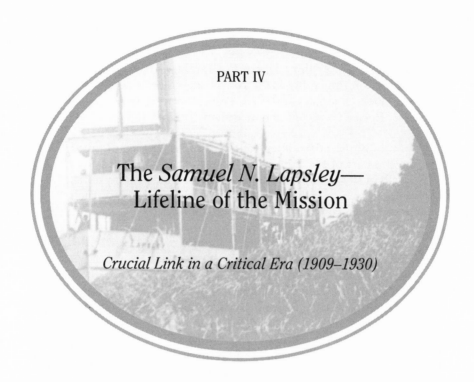

PART IV

The *Samuel N. Lapsley*— Lifeline of the Mission

Crucial Link in a Critical Era (1909–1930)

"The Scramble for Africa"[1]
1876–1912

IN HIS BOOK, *THE SCRAMBLE FOR AFRICA, THE WHITE Man's Conquest of the Dark Continent from 1876 to 1912*, Thomas Pakenham masterfully summarizes what happened to the African continent within that time frame:

> The Scramble for Africa is one of the most extraordinary phenomena in history. In 1880 most of the continent was still ruled by its inhabitants and was barely explored. Yet by 1902, five European powers—Britain, France, Germany, Belgium and Italy—had grabbed almost all of its ten million square miles, awarding themselves thirty new colonies and protectorates, and 110 million bewildered new subjects.

The sudden race for African territory swept the political masters of Europe off of their feet. The British colonist secretary protested this "absurd scramble." The German chancellor, Prince Bismarck, complained that he was being led into a "colonial whirl." The French prime minister called it a "steeple chase into the unknown."

Ironically, the provocation for this massive display of greed on the part of the European powers came from the heroic death in 1873 of the missionary-explorer David Livingstone, who had exposed the horrors of the African slave trade then in progress. His call for Africa to be redeemed by the "three C's"—Commerce, Christianity and Civilization—was aimed at the conscience of the civilized world. However, the initial response came from rival colonial enthusiasts in Europe. There were journalists like Henry Stanley, mariners like Pierre de Brazza, soldiers like Edward Lugard, pedagogues like Karl Peters, and gold-and-diamond tycoons like Cecil Rhodes.

At first the governments of Europe attempted to remain aloof from this race, for there seemed little to gain from the expense of building new empires in the desert or in malarial bush and swamp. But Europe was experiencing a period of economic stagnation, and Black Africa might be—as parts of South Africa had already proven—an El Dorado, a huge new market and tropical treasure house. Soon colonial fever swept the Continent, and the acquisition of overseas empire became identified with national prestige.

As the Scramble gathered momentum, a fourth "C"— Conquest—became dominant. The Maxim machine gun, rather than trade or the Cross, became the symbol of the age. In many colonies atrocities were commonplace and Africans were treated no better than animals. At the center of it all, cunningly exploiting the rivalries around him stood one enigmatic individual controlling the heart of the Dark Continent: Leopold II, king of the Belgians and personal owner of the Congo State.[2]

"Il faut a la Belgique une colonie!"
1876–1890

"Belgium *must* have a colony!" This was the consuming passion of King Leopold II. His Majesty's worldwide search for a large, lucrative colonial possession for Belgium eventually turned to Africa. In September 1876, he convened a conference of explorers and geographical experts with firsthand knowledge of the continent. Of this group, the king was particularly impressed with Verney Cameron, the British explorer who was the first man to cross Central Africa from east to west. Cameron described enthusiastically the astounding wealth of the natural resources of the whole area, observed during his three-year trek (1872–1875).[3]

Out of this conference emerged the International African Association of which the king himself was the permanent president, with the general secretary in his employ. The stated goal of this new organization was the suppression of the new wave of Arab-controlled slave trading spreading like wildfire across Central Africa from the east. His Majesty magnanimously offered to underwrite personally this noble crusade. At the same time, he commented privately to his ambassador to Great Britain, "I do not want to miss a chance in getting us a slice of the magnificent African cake!"[4]

Now in King Leopold's employ, Henry M. Stanley sailed for the Congo in February 1879. His specific assignment was to lay claim to the Lower Congo and strategic Stanley Pool for Belgium. He was to accomplish this by constructing a wagon road through the tortuous terrain of the Crystal Mountains from Matadi to the Pool, bypassing the two-hundred-mile-long series of thirty-two gigantic cataracts of the Congo River. Four model stations were to be established along the way, the fourth one at the base of the Pool itself, to be called Leopoldville, in honor of the king.[5]

By 1882 this unbelievably arduous engineering task was complete, at the cost of tons of dynamite and thousands of human lives, both black and white. At the same time, Stanley and King Leopold's agents were making treaties with the chiefs of the various ethnic groups through whose lands the new road passed.

These treaties gave the king exclusive rights to exploit the natural resources of all that area.[6]

The Berlin Conference on West Africa in 1884 recognized the International Association's control of the Congo basin. On July 1, 1885, the Congo Free State (*L'Etat Independent du Congo*) was established; its symbol was the blue standard with a single gold star in the center. According to the General Act of Berlin, signed on February 26, traders of every nation were to be free to compete commercially in the new colony.[7] In 1891, Leopold secretly ordered his agents that from then on all ivory was to be bought only for the state. Other orders followed, banning the harvesting of wild rubber, unless sold to the state. A new decree declared that all land belonged to the state except that specifically under native cultivation. In this way, the Congo Free State became a state monopoly.[8]

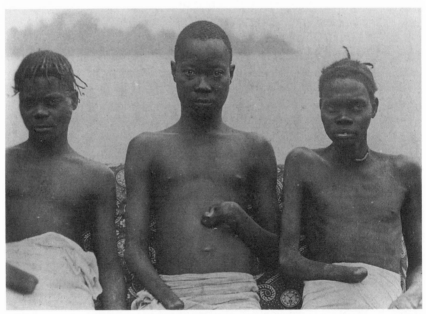

Chopping off of hands was one of the forms of punishment inflicted on those who failed to bring in their quota of raw rubber. Pictures such as this one were taken by Mr. Vass in order to document and publicize what was actually going on in the Congo Free State. Courtesy—Department of History, PCUSA, Montreat, North Carolina.

The representatives of the middle "C," the most important of David Livingstone's "Three C's—Commerce, Christianity, and Civilization," were the first to be aware of the inevitably tragic results of giving full sway to such a monopolistic regime. Dark, cruel, and greedy elements of human nature quickly surface when unrestricted by moderation, self-control, or true religious conviction. Rumors of "atrocities," barbaric forms of coercion and punishment practiced by Congo Free State agents and their henchmen, began to trickle into the international media. Were they true? The missionaries working among the oppressed people knew the tragic truth from firsthand experience. There was also confirmation from secular sources.

> *Were* the atrocity stories true? In 1899, after ten years, Morel, the leading British authority on West Africa, found it hard to say. . . . While laboring over the desiccated statistics of the Free State, he suddenly stumbled on an amazing discovery. He saw what the humanitarians had never guessed—that the King had had the trade figures doctored. Morel compared the official figures with the Elder Dempster shipping returns and the sale of rubber by the Free State and its concessionary companies on the Antwerp market. The real figure for exports must be much higher than the figures given and much higher than the figure for imports. Clearly the Free State officials were not paying the natives to bring the rubber from the jungle, nor were the natives doing it for love. The officials must be using forced labor, beating and shooting the rubber out of them. This meant that, if anything, the humanitarians had underestimated the abuses. These were not haphazard, but systematic. In short, the King's philanthropy was founded on "legalized robbery enforced by violence."[9]

Missionary Protesters of a Brutal Regime of Exploitation 1903–1909

As legal representative of the American Presbyterian Congo Mission, it was Dr. William M. Morrison's responsibility to report instances of abuse to Congo Free State authorities. Copies of mission correspondence during the years 1903–1909 contain many letters of complaint, citing actual cases of the obvious failure of the state to conform to the humanitarian limits placed upon it by the Berlin Treaty. Captain Vass's personal correspondence with Edward Morel, founder of the Congo Reform Association, was a steady source of documented information on the harsh practices of the "concessionaire companies," of which the Free State held controlling interest. Though grosser forms of oppression were sometimes less frequent, subtler forms of cruel force were observed among the people of the Kasai area where the mission worked. The missionaries realized that the only way change could come about would be by arousing public opinion and sentiment.

On June 20, 1903, Morrison had written to King Leopold II himself:

> I can assure Your Majesty that nothing has ever given me greater pain than to be compelled to lose confidence in the government's real desire to do justice according to the spirit of the Treaties of Berlin and Brussels, and it is after the most careful deliberation that I have reached the conclusion that our only hope lies in arousing the public opinion of the world against the iniquities which you know that your system must produce in Africa. I have lived under that unfortunate government for over six years. I have suffered myself, and I have seen the natives and traders suffer; and you treat those sufferings with disdain, though all the while making protestations of philanthropy and virtue. If you are really desirous of having me tell you the same things which I have told in London and will tell in Washington, I place myself at your disposition.[10]

On his way to the United States that year, he had stopped in London and addressed the Aborigines Protective Society, a public meeting in Whitehall and the Houses of Parliament,[11] making such an impact on his audiences that Edmond Morel named him, "Mr. Valiant for Truths of the Congo." Arriving in the United States, he bombarded the newspapers and magazines with articles such as, "The Mis-government of the Congo Free State." He addressed many large audiences throughout the country, as well as the Boston Peace Congress assembled in 1904.[12]

After his return to the mission field, where conditions had not improved, Dr. Morrison continued his steady pressure on the regime. In January 1908, he published in the mission's periodical, the *Kasai Herald*, a short, factual description written by Dr. Sheppard, of the actual conditions that he was daily observing among the Bakuba. As a result of this article, the British government sent their Congo consul, Mr. Wilfred G. Thesiger, to make a tour of the Bakuba area, investigating the complaints of armed force, of beating with lengths of hippo hide, called "chicots," of imprisonment, and of wanton destruction of rubber vines. The consul's report was sent from Boma in September 1908. His document, later presented to both Houses of the British Parliament, stated that he had found:

> (1) waste of natural resources in the cutting instead of tapping of the rubber vines; (2) taxing of villages a fixed number of rubber balls per month, with shortages punished by fines, imprisonment and use of the *chicot*; (3) armed *kapitas* (native overseers) in almost every village who must be supplied gratis with "food, palm wine, a house and a woman"; (4) use of the *Lukenga* and his soldiers to enforce the rubber tax and fines. Public feeling aroused by the report ran so high that stock of the Kasai Rubber Company suffered a severe slump.[13]

Years of pressure on Leopold's regime and such authenticated reports as Thesiger's finally produced results. On November 15, 1908, the Congo Free State became the Belgian Congo.

After the publication of Thesiger's report, the Company Kasai, which had the rubber monopoly in that area, demanded that an apologetic denial and retraction of Dr. Sheppard's article in the *Kasai Herald* be made by the writer and by the editor in the next issue of that publication. Dr. Morrison's reply to this demand was:

> We do not blame, personally, the individual agents and officials of your Company, except in so far as they may purposely misrepresent the facts, but we do and must

condemn this whole monopolistic system by which the
country is being ruthlessly stripped of its natural products,
with the natives getting but little return—your Company, in
the meanwhile, paying to its stockholders enormous divi-
dends, if the available figures are correct.[14]

In response to Morrison's letter, the Company Kasai promptly
brought action for libel against Morrison and Sheppard. The
summons dated February 23, 1909, alleged that Sheppard's article,
written a year before, contained lying affirmations very damaging
to the plaintiff and asked for eighty thousand francs in damages.
The two missionaries were to appear in Leopoldville on May 25,
1909. Thomas Chalmers Vinson, author of Morrison's biography,
explains the problem this presented:

> The trial was set for May 25th, after the beginning of the dry
> season. . . . The only means the missionaries had of reaching
> the scene of the trial was river steamer. The dry season
> commences about May 1, at which time the smaller rivers,
> such as the Lulua, fall very rapidly, making navigation most
> difficult. In those days no vessel of any description
> attempted to reach Luebo after the beginning of the dry
> season, communication with the outside world being cut off.
> The *Lapsley* has a very deep draught and never attempts to
> get in or out of Luebo between May 1st and October 1st.
>
> Notwithstanding these difficulties, they were warned by the
> Court that in the event they should, for any reason, fail to
> appear at the appointed hour, the trial would proceed
> without them and the judgment would be rendered.[15]

The Sheppard-Morrison Trial for Libel at Leopoldville
September 30, 1909

After receiving the court summons from Leopoldville,
Morrison and Sheppard in desperation tried the *Lapsley* as their

only possible means of transportation, but to no avail. It was evident that the only way the accused could make the nine-hundred-mile journey was to trek overland two hundred miles by hammock caravan to Bena Makima, the nearest river point on the Kasai. Twenty Bakuba witnesses from eleven different villages would have to make the journey with them downriver, traveling by canoe or river steamer, as passage became available.[16]

Meanwhile, the written request from Morrison to the United States consul to the Congo, William H. Handley, was also on its slow way downriver asking him, if he possibly could, to arrange a postponement of the trial. Back in the United States, Dr. S. H. Chester, the executive secretary of the Foreign Missions Committee of the Presbyterian Church, U.S., was doing all in his power. Trips to Washington resulted in a cable being sent by the state department to Brussels, requesting a postponement of the trial to September 30, 1909. Belgian Congo authorities were also warned by the United States secretary of state, Philander C. Knox, that a just and fair trial should be accorded the two American missionaries.[17]

Providentially, while the Morrison-Sheppard-Bakuba witness party was still en route to Leopoldville, the Company Kasai also agreed to a postponement because their counsel for the trial had not yet arrived from Brussels. Dr. Morrison found out about this only after his arrival in Leopoldville.[18]

In the meantime in England, Robert Whyte and Edmond Morel secured the legal services of the Honorable Emil Vandervelde, the famous Belgian Socialist Party leader, as the defendants' advocate.[19] For years, this man stood almost alone in his country, defending the rights of the native peoples of the Congo against the spoliation regime of King Leopold. Rev. T. C. Vinson recorded his response:

> Mr. Vandervelde welcomed this opportunity of investigating personally the conditions in the Congo. He gladly laid aside his official duties to make the long journey to Leopoldville, in order to see that justice was meted out.

When he was preparing to sail for the Congo, someone
reproached him for leaving his official duties and going so
far to defend "strangers"; to which he replied in words
worthy to be remembered: "No man is a stranger in a court
of Justice!"[20]

On October 4, 1909, Dr. Morrison and Dr. Sheppard were
acquitted by the tribunal responsible for the decision, there being
no "trial by jury" in Belgian jurisprudence.[21]

Morrison praised highly the integrity of the Italian judge,
M. Granpetrie, and described Vandervelde's line of argument:

M. Vandervelde's speech in our defense was a masterpiece
of eloquence, invincible logic, and pathetic appeal for justice
to be done for missionaries and especially the natives. The
chief points in his line of argument were that in the article
published in the *Kasai Herald* no injury was intended against
the Rubber Company. The attempt was simply to describe
existing conditions which we had a perfect right to do. It
was in fact our *duty*![22]

Dr. Morrison expressed warm gratitude to Vandervelde for his
refusal to accept any remuneration for his legal services. He

*Dr. William Morrison (left) and Dr. William Sheppard (right) stand with Bakuba
witnesses who journeyed to Kinshasa for the Sheppard-Morrison trial for libel.
Courtesy—Department of History, PCUSA, Montreat, North Carolina.*

thanked Consul Handley for his splendid diplomatic support and that of the State Department in Washington, activated by the many contacts made by Dr. S. H. Chester of the home Church. Rev. T. Hope Morgan, the manager of the mission's business affairs in Leopoldville had been of inestimable value. Mr. Robert Whyte and Mr. Edmond Morel were the ones who had secured Vandervelde's services. Hundreds of Christians in England, the United States, and the Congo had prayed unceasingly for the outcome of the trial. Most of all, Morrison and Sheppard appreciated the twenty Bakuba witnesses who grew weary during the long weeks of waiting so far from home. The entire party was gone for five long months, April through October 1909. The Company Kasai lawyer refused to let any of these witnesses testify at the trial, so their tedious, protracted journey and absence had seemingly been in vain.[23]

On December 14, 1909, King Leopold II of Belgium died. He was succeeded by his nephew, King Albert, who took most seriously his responsibility for restoring free trade and fair, humanitarian principles of government to the indigenous peoples of the Belgian Congo.

The Scottish Captain Takes Command
1908–1915

William Brown Scott, the second full-time *Lapsley* captain, was born in Glasgow, Scotland, of parents "both of whom were Scotch as far back as can be traced." At the age of thirteen, because of a father who was "more fond of sport and enjoying himself than caring for his children," he stopped school and began to work as an apprentice mechanic to support his family. In 1889, at the age of twenty-one, he "yielded himself to God, in answer to his mother's prayers and without anyone knowing about it." He immediately joined the YMCA Missionary Society and began to prepare for

missionary service by intensive Bible study and by becoming more
expert at his trade. He benefited especially from a medical class
that three dedicated Glasgow doctors arranged for anyone anticipating missionary service.[24]

In September 1905, Rev. Lachlan Vass, having signed the contract
for the *Lapsley* with Lobnitz & Company, Limited, Shipbuilders,
Renfrew, Scotland, began his search for a man who would be willing
to go with him to the Congo Free State to help reassemble and run
the stern-wheeler. On inquiring, Vass was referred to the Missionary
Society of the YMCA, where he was introduced to and interviewed
Scott. So impressed was Captain Vass that he urged him to apply at
once to the Board of World Missions. In November 1905, William
Scott was accepted as a missionary to the Congo Free State. The
Scottish mechanic sailed with Vass and the crated steamer
Philippeville to Matadi. In the steamy heat of Stanley Pool he toiled
with Vass and the Congolese and West African workmen to
reassemble the beautiful little paddle wheeler into a real, "living"
river personality.[25]

On January 22, 1909, Captain Scott left Luebo on the *Lapsley*,
taking Vass on the first lap of his final journey back to the United
States. Months of unremitting malarial fevers had so weakened the
first captain that his resignation seemed advisable. The Siegs and
Motte Martins were waiting at Leopoldville, so a return trip to
Luebo was made as soon as possible. Mr. Guiton of the Congo
Balolo Mission was also aboard. He had the distinction of being
the very first visitor from a sister Congo mission to visit Luebo.[26]

A copy of the ship's log sent by Scott to Vass early in June 1909
showed that the next upriver trip from April 26 to May 20 was an
unusually slow one, taking twenty-five days. The water level was
already dropping rapidly as the dry season approached; there was
considerable difficulty with sandbanks; and well-stocked wooding
stops were hard to find.

Distinguished passenger on this trip was British Consul
Thesiger, who had been instructed to tour the Bakuba country,
investigating the condition of the people and the methods of the
Company Kasai. After returning to Luebo, Thesiger was to make a
second tour through Lulua country to Luluabourg. From there he

was to proceed to Lusambo and return by steamer to his consular post to report his findings to the British government.[26] These diplomatic instructions to Thesiger were the direct result of British Foreign Office authorities' having read Sheppard's article in the January 1, 1908, issue of the *Kasai Herald*.[27]

A Hasty Decision Tests Scott's Character

The summons received by Sheppard and Morrison on May 20, 1909, had been issued by the Court of First Instance at Leopoldville on February 23 of that year. Sheppard, as author of the January 1, 1908, *Kasai Herald* article, and Morrison, as responsible editor, were both charged with libel against the Company Kasai. They were to report to the court in Leopoldville by May 25. In case of their failure to appear by that date, court proceedings would go ahead without them.[28]

As soon as the two missionaries had read the summons they had received, they called Scott and told him that he *must* take the *Lapsley immediately* back to Leopoldville! He was told to load cargo on Sunday, something never done before at Luebo, and leave on Monday. The captain explained that the water level was already too low even to consider a downriver trip at that time. He had no desire to repeat the experiences of "Stranded Camp." Desperate to get to Leopoldville because of the libel action, Morrison and Sheppard ordered Scott to get under way, regardless of navigational barriers. Against his will and better judgment, the captain reluctantly conceded. For three terrible days, he and his crew struggled over sandbanks, failing even to get out of the Lulua River and into the much larger Kasai. On the third day, Scott told the two missionaries that it was impossible to proceed; he turned his ship about and scraped, pushed, and pulled his way over the sandbanks back to Luebo.[29]

A hastily called mission meeting the next day on May 26, 1909, voted: "In view of the fact that the Mission has lost its entire confidence in Mr. Scott, it was moved and carried that he present his resignation to the Mission in writing."[30]

Scott requested and received permission to "make the usual repairs and overhauling of the steamer," but he was forbidden to make any alterations.[31]

It was Morrison's and Sheppard's utter frustration at this failure to respond to the legal summons to Leopoldville that led them to such a rash act. They later acutely regretted it and sincerely apologized for such a hasty reaction. Scott, on his part, was deeply hurt that his professional integrity and reputation were now suspect. It had even been broadly hinted that he had been *bribed* by the Company Kasai to refuse to make the trip.[32]

It took Morrison and Sheppard some time to gather witnesses willing to leave their tribal areas and travel to alien territory. It also took time to prepare the caravan for the nine-hundred-mile-long journey downriver. The first part would be on foot to the nearest port on the large Kasai River. The remainder of the trip would be by canoe or passing steamer. They had no choice, because of the low, dry-season water levels, but to make the long journey to Leopoldville in this way.

"Cracks" in "Earthen Vessels"

Fortunately, Scott's determination to serve his Lord as a missionary included a common-sense approach to human frailty. God's "clay pots," selected to contain and dispense his message of salvation to people, often have visible flaws. On mission stations where a small group of unusually strong-willed, highly motivated people are in daily, hourly contact, personality "rubs" and irritations often threaten unity of spirit and action. Friction points, however, can be eased by the oil of the Holy Spirit, and angry outbursts forgiven.

Even though Scott's forced resignation had been officially submitted as requested, the dry season isolation of Luebo kept him at his post. But even without this factor, he felt compelled to stand by his ship until another captain could replace him. News had come that E. D. Howard, a Londoner, was on his way to Luebo, to take over.[33] Quietly, patiently, Scott went about his daily work, releasing his feelings only in letters to "Dear Old Vass," with whom he had worked so well. Not only did he fill the hours with the necessary overhauling and repairs of the *Lapsley*, he also busied himself with a small sawmill bought for $175 from the American Baptist Missionary Union. Using the circular saw, planing machine, board saw, and lathe, he worked each day making door frames and screened windows and doors for the new burnt-brick residences. With proper screening for the missionaries' homes, the frightening frequency of malarial fevers might be lessened.[34]

The last week of August 1909 scattered thunderheads began to form and occasional dark curtains of rain swept along the horizon. With increasing frequency midnight storms thundered overhead; the sandbanks began to shrink and protruding rocks to disappear. By October the *Lapsley* was back in her native element, her clean, oiled 250-horsepower compound engines rumbling a steady bass.

Captain Scott assigns individual loads to porters, eager for work; smaller cargo items were balanced on the heads of the carriers as they climbed Luebo hill. Courtesy— Department of History, PCUSA, Montreat, North Carolina.

The pulsating splash of the stern-wheel provided a soprano accompaniment. An elation of worshiping praise filled Scott as his beloved *Lapsley* responded to the slightest turn by his hands on the ship's smooth steering wheel.

Throughout the 1909–1910 rainy season the Scottish captain continued to pilot the steamer. On November 26, the *Lapsley* arrived from Leopoldville with British Vice Consul Thurston aboard, and an English couple touring the Congo, the Ian McKenzies. E. D. Howard, under a one-year contract to the executive committee, was also a passenger, obviously expecting to take over the captaincy of the *Lapsley* immediately. Best of all, a brand new, much-needed iron tender was in tow, the gift of the Presbyterian Church of Charlotesville, Virginia.[35]

The May 7 arrival of the *Lapsley* brought the very first member of the Executive Committee of Foreign Missions and his wife to visit the Congo mission field, Dr. and Mrs. James O. Reavis. Dr. J. G. Pritchard, the mission's first dentist, was also aboard. The steamer mail conveyed the interesting rumor that the British vice consul might be stationed at Luebo.[36]

On two successive downriver trips Scott worked with Howard trying to communicate to him his own accumulated store of river-knowledge and his familiarity with the engines. It soon became apparent that the new recruit had no intention of getting his hands greasy; he never went down to the lower deck to familiarize himself with the engines. Also, it became obvious that he had never handled tools. Most frustrating of all to Scott was the fact that he always had a book in his hand. Even on the bridge while the ship was passing through swirling currents, deftly trying to avoid hidden rocks, he only glanced up when Scott asked him to observe, and then continued his reading.[37]

In July 1910, Scott returned to Scotland. Also aboard, returning to England, was E. D. Howard. More than ever aware of "cracked pots," Scott wrote to Vass, "God knows that I did my very best!"[38]

On September 6, 1910, the Executive Committee of Foreign Missions of the Presbyterian Church, U.S. reappointed William B. Scott, "formerly a member of the African Mission . . . as Captain of the *Lapsley* for the present year at an increased salary of $400."[39]

The American Presbyterian Congo Mission, at its annual mission meeting, voted on November 12, that same year:

> Moved and carried unanimously that we as a Mission have received with much satisfaction and appreciation, the information that the Executive Committee has arranged for Scott's definite return to the field. We heartily welcome him back to us and take this occasion to urge his attendance and free participation in all meetings of the Mission and station.[40]

"Two Are Better Than One"

Back home in Glasgow, William Scott had been experiencing one happy event after another. Not only had he been unexpectedly reappointed by the Presbyterian Church in the United States as a missionary, he also had become engaged to Miss Rachel Boyd, a Glasgow lassie.

By January 1911, Captain Scott was back at Luebo eagerly awaiting his fiancée's arrival. The editor of the January 1911 *Kasai Herald* wrote: "If the bride could have been sent out by wireless telegraphy, the happy pair would already have been made one!"[41]

Another joyful aspect of Scott's work at this time was that Dr. J. G. Pritchard, "the big-hearted jovial young dentist, standing six feet, two inches and weighing nearly 220 pounds, and possessing mental attainments to match his size," had become his eager assistant, quickly demonstrating a flair for handling the stern-wheeler. On any occasion, as needed, he also used his dental skills to bring relief to sufferers.[42]

In March the *Lapsley* captain was given permission by the mission to convert the ship's dining salon into a stateroom for use of passengers. He was also requested to stop when convenient for a couple of days at some of the mission's outposts along the river, to meet with the Christians to nurture and encourage them. A very real honor and responsibility was placed upon the captain and Dr. Pritchard when they were appointed to be the official representatives of the American Presbyterian Congo Mission to the Conference of Protestant Missions meeting at Bolenge on October 5, 1911.[43]

On May 26, 1911, Miss Boyd and Captain Scott were married at the Christian and Missionary Alliance station at Boma by Rev. John Whitehead of the Baptist Missionary Society. The couple had planned originally to be married at Matadi, but Scott was so eager to greet his bride that he procured a row boat and spent the night paddling downriver to Boma! Some of the passengers whom Miss Boyd had met on the *Leopoldville*, the steamer that had brought them all from Belgium, were present. Hooper, the chief engineer of that ocean steamer, also came to the wedding, as did the American vice consul and many Matadi missionaries.[44]

The caliber and spirit of the young lady who was now Mrs. Scott is evident in the description she wrote of her first introduction to the *Lapsley*, her "honeymoon ship":

> Wednesday morning we started on the train journey for Leopoldville, where we arrived on Thursday afternoon. We had the best reception of all here, as most of the steamship *Lapsley's* crew were at the station to meet us, and when we got to the beach, it was to find the steamer in beautiful order and nicely decorated with flags for the occasion. My first impression was that I would not find it a difficult matter to love the Baluba people; I was at once deeply interested in them. The *Lapsley* is a lovely steamer, and in comparison with the other mission steamers I have seen since coming out, has an easy first. I enjoyed my first Sunday very much. It was a delight to see all the crew gathered on deck at 9:30 a.m. to have their service. Mr. Scott conducted it, and one after another of the men got up to take part by prayer and speaking. Of course, they all take part in the singing. As I sat looking and listening, the words came to my mind, "Whosoever calleth on the name of the Lord shall be saved." So many of them through the mission at Luebo had called, and were now rejoicing in salvation.[45]

Not all first-trip-on-the-*Lapsley* experiences were as pleasant as those of Rachel Scott. Mrs. Alonzo Edmiston described early in 1912 one of the more somber aspects of the steamer's ministry up and down the river:

One day as we were approaching a trader's post on the bank of the river, two white men stood on the bank waving a white flag, asking our steamer to stop. When we had anchored, they came on board, quite excited, and said, "We have a very sick comrade, please help us to do something for him!" But while they were yet speaking, another came saying, "It is no use, he is dead!" It was indeed a sad occasion. The dead man was just twenty-five years of age and had been in the Congo only three months. After rendering what service we could to the bereaved parties, our boat went on its way.[46]

The *Lapsley* Goes Big-Game Hunting

Captain Scott, in an article he wrote for the *Missionary Survey*, revealed the more dangerous, adventurous side of operating the *Lapsley*:

As we neared the place where we intended stopping for the night we saw an elephant in the edge of the forest. By the marks on the trees, we knew there were many others around. After we landed, the wood cutters went off to their night's work. . . . Our cook came in, in great excitement, to say that there was an elephant near the steamer and asked permission for the man having the gun to fire at the animal. To our surprise, the bullet struck the elephant! In searching for the cause of his pain, he found the anchor and tried to trample it; next, he found a sheep tied to the anchor chain and killed it, and then made for the steamer. When only a few yards away, one of the men pulled a burning log out of the fire and struck the elephant on the head. The shower of sparks seemed to frighten him. He took to the river, going in just ahead of the steamer. You never saw such tossing of the water and a struggle to get up the bank! Finally, after several shots, the elephant was killed and sank. The men, after much diving, succeeded in finding the slain animal. By tying ropes to his legs they were able to pull him to the bank, and soon had about a ton of his flesh, and the head,

with the tusks. When we divided up the meat that afternoon, each man got about forty pounds. They were a happy
set of men and had great feasting. The ivory I gave to the
government, as I have not a license to kill elephants. I am
sure it will be a long time before we have another experience
in elephant hunting.[47]

The Preacher-Captain Comes Aboard
1912–1915

In the spring of 1912, Captain and Mrs. Scott were forced to
leave the mission on an emergency sick leave. Dr. Pritchard,
having completed a three-year term, returned permanently to the
United States to practice dentistry. Consequently, there was no one
on the mission capable of taking over the *Lapsley*.

Just before Scott left, the mission agreed to allow the *Lapsley* to
be chartered to the British government during the dry season
months of July, August, and September of that year. The purpose
of the charter was a tour of the Upper Congo waterways by the
British Consul, Mr. Lamont, and the American Consul at Boma,
Mr. Hazelton. Agreeing to the charter was a favor the mission was
glad to give, for the British and American consulates had been most
sympathetic and cooperative in rendering help with difficulties
with the Congo State. The mission steamer could not be used on the
Lulua River out of Luebo during those months anyway.[48]

The British consulate insured the steamer for £1,100 and
promised to pay $1000 and all expenses for the use of the steamer
during the agreed months. The only stipulation the mission placed
upon the charter was that the steamer should maintain its known
character up and down the river as "The Steamer of God." It was
not to be run on Sundays and the regular services of worship were
to be held on board for the crew.[49]

In March 1912, an urgent call was sent by the executive
committee to a young Union Theological Seminary student to go to
the Belgian Congo and serve as *Lapsley* captain. Someone had
informed the committee that Arch C. McKinnon had had experience

with machinery and steam power and had operated a steamboat on the Arkansas River! As a result, by July 24, Reverend Mr. McKinnon, just ordained as a minister by his Arkansas Presbytery, and his wife, Eva King McKinnon, were aboard the *Mauretania* on their way to Africa.[50]

After several months under a doctor's care in Glasgow, William Scott was enough improved to travel by train to London to talk to young McKinnon about all that was involved in the work of captaincy of the *Lapsley*. McKinnon was delighted to have first-hand pointers on the difficult job that awaited him at Stanley Pool.[51] His description of his first reaction to the unimpressive sight of his crew, followed by his increasing respect for them and their capabilities is interesting to note:

> I wondered when I came face to face with these strangers who made up the crew of the *Lapsley* whether I had made a mistake in attempting to answer this emergency call. They did not look as if they knew how to run a steamboat, even with someone to tell them what to do. This little wave of fear did not last long, however, when I saw how these men responded to the various duties and responsibilities assigned to them. The two pilots, Muloki and Lumami, had had several years of experience guiding this *Lapsley* and seemed to know just which parts of the river would be safe for our passage. They knew the most dangerous places to be avoided.

> On the third day up the main Congo River, Muloki pointed to a whirling back current just below a sharp bend in the river and said, "There's where the first *Lapsley* capsized and sank."

> Our native engineer, whose name was Hammond, came to the Congo from the British Colony of Sierra Leone on the west coast of Africa, a thousand miles or so north of the Congo. He had learned what he knew about steam engines in a colonial vocational school before coming to the Congo. He also had been one of the assistant engineers on one of the river steamers of the Lever Brothers' Soap Company before

joining the *Lapsley* crew. He was very dependable and careful to see that the *Lapsley's* engines were kept clean and well oiled.

He was also a big help as an interpreter before I learned the native language. His command of English was not up to classical standards, but he could always make himself understood in English. He had also acquired a smattering of several of the Congo dialects, which helped all of us in our contacts with the native village people along the river.

My admiration for the various members of the *Lapsley* crew increased markedly from what I had thought of them in the beginning. Even the wood-cutters, just ordinary workmen, with no special skills, were worthy of praise for the manner in which they hustled out from the steamer when we stopped for wood.[52]

The Preacher-Captain Lives Up to His Name

Members of the Luebo station church took pride in giving a suitable Tshiluba language name to each of their new missionaries. Because he was an ordained minister who had been specifically called to take charge of the *Lapsley*, McKinnon was given the name, *Muambi Kapitene*, the "Preacher-Captain."[53]

Twice during his first upriver trips, McKinnon had to turn the stern-wheeler abruptly about and go back downriver. The first occasion was the serious illness of the wife of Dr. Llewellyn Coppedge, the first and only doctor the mission had. The Coppedges had made the nine-hundred-mile trip on the *Lapsley* to the nearest dentist at the Swedish Baptist mission in Brazzaville. On their return trip, the *Lapsley* had reached Dima, on the Kasai River, when Coralie Coppedge's illness became so critical that an immediate return to Leopoldville became imperative. The Coppedges were forced to return to the United States. When Mrs. Coppedge regained her health, the doctor and his wife became medical missionaries to Mexico (1920–1948).[54]

The second "right, about face" of the *Lapsley* had a better outcome, which Captain McKinnon himself described:

> One of the crew on the lower deck stooped over by the side of the boat to dip up a bucket of water from the river. He did not realize that the speed of the boat would cause a strong pull on the bucket when it was full. The pull was strong enough to cause him to fall overboard.
>
> In his excitement he did not look for the nearest land and start swimming to it. Instead, he swam up-stream towards the steamer. By the time the alarm reached the bridge, he looked like a small object floating in the waters.
>
> We turned the steamer around and made full speed back to him before his strength gave out. When we came within a few yards of him, we stopped the engine and allowed the steamer to float within his reach. He still had strength enough to grab hold of one of the brace rods and hold on until the men on board could reach down and drag him to safety again. He was unharmed from the long swim but was very much frightened.
>
> Most of these steamer men were good swimmers and this one was unusually good. But he was very fortunate not to have been picked up by one of the big crocodiles that made headquarters in that particular section of the Kasai River.[55]

McKinnon's pride in and care for the *Lapsley* is evident in his arranging for the mission steamer to be placed in dry dock at Dima, the rubber company post, for repainting:

> Our equipment at Luebo did not include a slip to pull the steamer out of the water, but we had a fairly complete repair shop in other respects. When we arrived at Dima, we found that the slip had been made ready, so we had the *Lapsley* out of the water in a very little while. The slip was made of railroad rails embedded in concrete and reaching out into the river some distance and leading up the bank at a thirty-five

degree angle. It was a bit uncomfortable to be living on the boat at that angle for the next two weeks while the repair work was being done. But that was our home for the time being, so we made the best of it.

Our men, with the repair crew of the rubber company, got out their tools and began scraping the hull to get the old paint and the rust off before applying a new coat of paint. We had brought along the paint from our supply store at Luebo and as soon as the hull was clean, our men applied a fresh coat of black marine paint on the whole surface. . . .

As soon as they finished painting the hull, they brought out a supply of white paint and spent the whole week "prettying" up the upper structure. They also re-varnished all the cabins both inside and out. With all this painting finished, the *Lapsley* looked like a new steamer!

While we were waiting for all this work to be done, our friends of the rubber company had their hunters bring us a generous portion of the meat they brought back from a day's chase. One day they sent us a whole quarter of a big hooded buffalo, which is very similar to our beef. These generous portions we always shared with our native crew. We had no means of refrigeration in those days and were glad that the crew could have this meat supplement. . . .[56]

The strong evangelical emphasis of McKinnon's captaincy is shown in the fact that while at Dima he took advantage of the opportunity to baptize twelve more candidates for baptism, leaving many others to be examined later. Thus, the thriving church at Dima was planted by the hand-in-hand navigational and evangelical ministries of the *Samuel N. Lapsley* and its Preacher-Captain.[57]

One other outstanding feature of McKinnon's captaincy was the setting of *Lapsley* records. During the 1912–1913 rainy season *six* round trips were made, breaking all previous records for speed and smooth maximum service to the American Presbyterian Congo Mission. Four had been the usual number made between

October and May. The greatest number of passengers had also been carried, twelve of them new missionaries, plus older ones returning to the field from home or sick leave, as well as personnel of other missions. Needless to say, the cabins were full and some slept on cots on the deck.[58]

A Floating Butcher Shop

Like Captains Vass and Scott, McKinnon occasionally had the problem of bringing elephant meat aboard. On a 1912 downriver trip, the crew spotted a dead elephant floating in the river and immediately sent an excited delegation to the captain requesting him to stop the steamer so that they could take advantage of this free supply of meat. Captain McKinnon related:

> I could see that the elephant was dead and that there would be no danger to the men if we did stop to get it. But I was afraid that the animal had been dead too long and that the meat on board would not be a pleasant traveling companion during the rest of the downriver voyage. When I told them that the elephant was dead, they said, "Truly, we already know he is dead, but we still want the meat!" I answered, "But the meat will have a strong odor." They replied, "That doesn't matter. We don't eat the odor, only the meat!"

Reluctantly, McKinnon turned the steamer about and pushed the lifeboat, full of elated crewmen, and the elephant which lashed alongside, to a nearby sandbank. There they spent the entire night cutting up the carcass and drying chunks of flesh over numerous, scattered bonfires. This smoking process effectively prevented the passengers from having to endure an obnoxious odor during the remainder of the voyage.

As the *Lapsley* neared the end of its downriver journey, the long-distance communication drums of the river-shore villages relayed the message of the approaching arrival of an abundant supply of dried elephant. A huge milling crowd of meat-hungry buyers, money in hand, awaited their arrival in Kinshasa, crowding the entire landing beach and even wading out into the water.[59]

The Opening of Lusambo Station

Luebo (1891) was the original founding station of the American Presbyterian Congo Mission, followed by Ibanche (1897) among the Bakuba, and Mutoto (1912) among the Lulua. The December 1912 mission meeting made a bold decision to open a fourth station at Lusambo, an important river port on the Sankuru River. The Sankuru is the largest tributary of the Kasai River, the Zaire River's biggest artery. Unlike Luebo's Lulua River, it is navigable the entire year up to and a little beyond Lusambo.[60]

Lusambo is famous in Zaire history. It was the base of military operations for stopping the encroachment of Arab-controlled slave-raiding parties coming into Central Africa from Zanzibar and the east coast. Even though many of the Belgian and Congolese soldiers who fought in those bloody battles were killed, "the Trade" was finally halted.[61]

Rev. R. D. Bedinger was appointed to select the right location for the new post. Its major qualifications were that it was to have good riverbank and beach positions for tying the *Lapsley* to the shore, a good fresh-water spring nearby, proximity to a main government tribunal, and a large native population which had already demonstrated an eagerness for the mission presence. The first site selected was rejected by the Belgian Congo officials because it was within an area reserved for native populations only. A second site was chosen which turned out to be far better than the first. It was higher in altitude, commanding a broad view of the Sankuru in both directions, was much cooler, and was more healthful than the first site selected.[62]

In August 1913, the McKinnons moved from Luebo to Lusambo, which became designated as the *Lapsley's* year-round base. Captain McKinnon described his new post as follows:

> Lusambo is located on the north bank of the Sankuru River, a few miles below the head of navigation. It is about 400 miles from where this stream empties into the Kasai, and

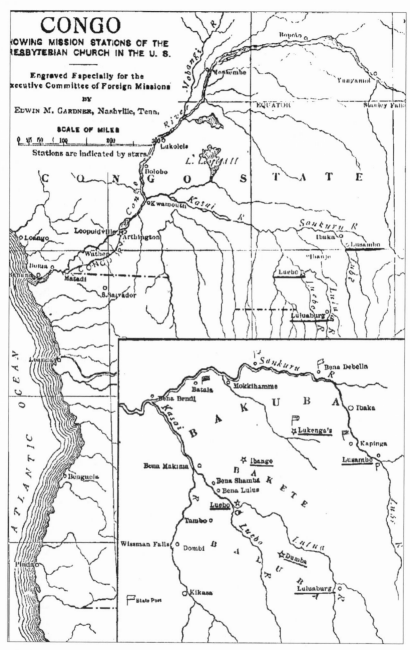

The inset map shows the Kasai, Lulua, and Sankuru River areas of the Zaire River system, at that time still called the "Congo." The location of Luebo, Lusambo, and Luluabourg are especially to be noted. From—The Missionary, May 1904, page 179. Courtesy—Department of History, PCUSA, Montreat, North Carolina.

about 550 miles from Luebo by river, though it is only about half this distance over land. It is the capital of the Kasai District, though the District is soon to be divided and this will become the Sankuru District, while Luebo will be made the capital of the Kasai District. There are, at present, about 75 or 80 state officials and other white residents in the place, with about ten houses of merchandise which do a general business on the order of our country stores at home. The native population, in and around Lusambo, is estimated at about 40,000, though no accurate census has ever been taken.

Our station, which covers an area of 330 feet square, is located nearly two miles up the river from the government buildings and the business section of the place, and is surrounded on all sides by large villages, though the main bulk of them are between us and the Seat of Justice. The river is only one hundred yards down a gradual slope from the front of the Mission property, while behind the station the elevation gradually increases until it reaches about three hundred feet a few hundred yards back. The tall rock cliffs just across the river are beautiful, and the hills behind and above them, with their fresh green covering of grass and tropical palms are especially pleasant to look upon.[63]

New Features of the *Lapsley's* Operation

The developing aspects of the services rendered by the *Lapsley* were clearly evident by 1913. Operation of the mission steamer began to require "red tape." Licenses had to be purchased for all "wooding stations" regularly visited for firewood for the boiler.[64]

Use of river navigational maps became more sophisticated as the *Lapsley's* captains were requested to report seasonal changes in the shifting patterns of the river currents. Appearances or disappearances of sandbanks after rainy season flooding were to be noted as well as any observations on recognized, dangerous underwater rock formations that threatened unwary vessels.[65]

A list of approximate sailing dates was being compiled for distribution to interested parties up and down the Kasai River. On each downriver trip, a telegram was sent from Kwamouth to the Congo Balolo Mission in Kinshasa, operators of the Union Mission House, a welcoming hostel for incoming and outgoing personnel of all missions working in the Belgian Congo, so the host could be informed ahead of time how many *Lapsley* passengers could be expected.

Also, an expense account of all disbursements made was required to be given to the mission treasurer at Luebo after each trip. In addition, rules governed the drawing up of "shopping lists" given to the captain for purchases to be made in the Kinshasa stores.[66]

Ecumenical Aspects of the *Lapsley's* Services

The transfer of the American Presbyterian Congo Mission's main riverbase from Luebo to Lusambo significantly strengthened an already warm and broadly cooperative relationship with other missions.

Dr. William McCutchan Morrison did much to establish a truly ecumenical basis for all Protestant mission work in the Belgian Congo. Dr. du Plissis, leader of the Dutch Reformed Church in South Africa, characterized Dr. Morrison as

> . . . no narrow sectarian. The little pool of his own denomination was submerged beneath the flowing tide of his broad humanity and warm-hearted Christianity. He belonged not to *a* church, but to *the* church. He was a missionary not of the American Presbyterian Congo Mission, but of Christ; he called no man lord, but all men brothers.[67]

Dr. Morrison's biographer, the Reverend Chalmers Vinson, wrote of him:

> He kept the map of Africa constantly before his eyes. He mapped out the field for which our own church had assumed responsibility and endeavored to select the places of strategic importance for the location of mission stations.

He studied the tribes immediately contiguous to our territory and endeavored to induce other denominations to take
up the task of evangelization.

He was convinced that the overlapping of different denominations
in their efforts, when there were vast areas unoccupied, was "a
selfish waste of energy and contrary to the mind and will of
Christ."[68]

With this flexible principle to guide him, Dr. Morrison corre-
sponded with the Reverend Henri Anet, head of the organization
of evangelical churches of Belgium. He urged Belgian Protestants
to select a field of missionary activity in their own colony. In
response to this plea, an unoccupied region near Tshofa on the
Lomami River, northeast of the Presbyterian mission area, was
selected and a concession granted for occupation.[69]

A heartwarming example of gracious hospitality offered the
Lapsley's crew by a sister mission is evident in McKinnon's description of Christmas 1912, spent in Kinshasa:

> We finished all our business affairs and had the *Lapsley*
> loaded by December 24th, but the missionaries at Kinshasa
> invited us over for the Christmas festivities and the celebra-
> tion of our Lord's birthday. They were members of the
> British Missionary Society. We moved the *Lapsley* to their
> landing beach and spent two days with them. They
> prepared a big Christmas dinner and invited a number of
> their business friends in to enjoy it with us. Their native
> Christians who lived nearby did all they could to make our
> steamer men enjoy the holiday.[70]

The *Lapsley* made another very real ecumenical contribution by
helping Mennonites launch their Congo Inland Mission, west of
Luebo. On March 12, 1911, the Defenseless (Pacifist) and the
Central Mennonite Conferences had united to form the United
Mennonite Board of Missions. Dr. William Sheppard, cofounder of
the American Presbyterian Congo Mission, on home leave at that
time, had met with this board in Bloomington, Illinois, and urged
them to occupy the large unoccupied area adjacent to Luebo on the

west. Home of Baluba, Batshioko, and Bampende, no work, neither Catholic nor Protestant, was being done there. Other advantages were the availability of the *Lapsley* for transportation of personnel and freight and Dr. Morrison's Tshiluba grammar and dictionary for immediate language study. Because of its proximity to Luebo, the people of this area were begging for teachers and evangelists.[71]

In January 1912, Rev. and Mrs. L. B. Haigh began the difficult task of surveying the territory and selecting sites at Kalamba and at Djoko Punda on the Kasai River, the latter to serve as transport station for the Congo Inland Mission. Now, new recruits were desperately needed.[72]

Early on December 26, 1912, while Captain McKinnon was at Kinshasa "getting up steam" for the *Lapsley's* boiler, the Jensens, Mr. Herr, and Miss Kroker came aboard for the upriver journey.[73] After a time of observation of the work at Luebo, on January 23, 1913, these new Mennonite missionaries of the Congo Inland Mission completed their journey to Djoko Punda on the *Lapsley*.[74]

A most creative and congenial partnership has continued over the years between the adjoining Congo Inland Mission and American Presbyterian Congo Mission, particularly in the field of writing and publishing a wide variety of Christian literature for the use of Tshiluba-speaking churches. The Tshiluba Literature Committee, with African and missionary personnel from both missions, has processed and approved assigned manuscripts, printed at the J. Leighton Wilson Printing Press at Luebo. These have been sold in mission bookshops all over Zaire.

Methodist Bishop Lambuth's First Journey to the Congo

By August 1913, Captain W. B. Scott had recovered enough to be able to return alone to Luebo; his wife, Rachel, rejoined him in May 1914. They were active in the operation of the *Lapsley* for only a year and a half. Then, in 1915, tropical illnesses once again took their toll and this gifted couple had to return to their native Scotland permanently.[75]

.

That year and a half, however, was a particularly crucial and interesting period in the mission steamer's usefulness. Captain Scott and the *Lapsley* had the high privilege of being major factors in the establishment of the neighboring mission of the Methodist Episcopal Church South.

In 1891, Dr. Walter R. Lambuth, the bishop of the Church, had offered himself to its board of missions to select a site for work in the Congo Free State.[76] As early as 1892, the Presbyterian Church in the United States had urged their Methodist brothers to join them in the new endeavors just started by Lapsley and Sheppard.[77]

But it was only in the fall of 1910 that the bishop, by then the secretary of the Methodist Foreign Mission Committee, was sent to Luebo to consult with Dr. William Morrison in regard to the selection of a mission field. Without hesitation, he was directed to the great untouched ethnic group called the Batetela, northeast of Lusambo. At that time, Luebo missionaries supplied Bishop Lambuth and Dr. John Wesley Paine, his African-American companion, with everything necessary for the long caravan journey to the Batetela area. Forty carriers had been secured, but sixty were needed. After an appeal to the Luebo Church by Dr. Morrison, Ruling Elder Mudimbi and twenty-two Luebo Christians volunteered to complete the needed number of carriers. God's providence was wonderfully evident in Elder Mudimbi's willingness to accompany the Methodists on this journey. He was one of the many boys who had been sold into slavery who were lovingly redeemed by Luebo missionaries then adopted, reared, and schooled by the missionaries into maturity. The elder, also an evangelist, had been one of several children brought by slavers from the Batetela area to sell in the Luebo market.

Bishop Lambuth himself recounted what happened on this eventful journey:

> On December 22, 1911, we started from Luebo overland on our tour of exploration, with sixty carriers who bore our tent, hammocks, provisions, cloth, salt, medicine chest, type-writer, etc. Our "pocket book" consisted of sixteen sacks of

trade salt and many bolts of cloth, money being of no value in the remote interior. . . . We crossed many rivers and streams, waded through swamps, met numerous chiefs, visited countless villages, treated some four hundred patients, were exposed to malarial fever and bitten a number of times by tsetse flies, but by the goodness and mercy of God, we escaped all these dangers and, penetrating to the heart of Batetela country, arrived at the village of the great chief, Wembo Nyama, on Thursday, February 1, 1912.

At first, the chief, who was the largest man we met in all our travels, was distant and suspicious, but suddenly his whole demeanor changed. He could not conceal his joy! He had discovered a long-lost friend in Mudimbi, the evangelist, whom he had not seen for nearly twenty years and whose father was also a chief who had been shot in a wild raid on his village. Then our converted cannibal cook turned out to be another friend of his boyhood days!

The chief had assigned us to an indifferent house on the side of the street. He now took us to his own house and, ordering his servants to bring out the biggest goat in the village, two baskets of rice, one of yams and an abundance of fruit, made us at home.

We remained four days, and at his urgent request to return, we determined to open the new mission in or near his village, believing that the hand of God had shaped our course and raised up a friend.[78]

Bishop Lambuth promised the chief that he would try to secure a concession for a mission station and return with personnel to staff it by the eighteenth month. Wembo Nyama replied that he would be "cutting notches on a stick, one for each moon, until the eighteenth notch had been reached, when he would expect their shadows to fall on the ground at the full moon, by the side of his shadow."

Arriving back in the United States, Bishop Lambuth found that his official duties demanded a trip to South America. He realized that it would be impossible to return to Wembo Nyama by the eighteenth month. So he wrote to Luebo requesting that a message be sent at once to Wembo Nyama to explain the delay and promising to come back by the twenty-fourth moon.[79]

Establishment of the Methodist Episcopal Congo Mission

The blessed unimportance of maintaining rigid denominational lines in missionary outreach is beautifully demonstrated in the opening of Methodist work among the Batetela of Zaire.

True to his word, Bishop Lambuth left Antwerp on November 8, 1913, with the promised personnel for launching the work of the Methodist Church at Wembo Nyama. They were Dr. and Mrs. R. L. Mumpower, a physician and nurse couple, with their baby, Elizabeth; Rev. and Mrs. C. C. Bush, a minister and teacher combination; and Mr. and Mrs. J. A. Stockwell, a builder and agriculturalist, whose wife was also a teacher. What a wonderful team with which to start a new mission![80]

Dr. William M. Morrison, who had been in the United States on home leave, was with them, returning to his field. On this voyage, Dr. Morrison held daily shipboard sessions with the new recruits. Bishop Lambuth exulted: "The practical knowledge the new missionaries received from these lectures was worth more than two years of actual experience on the field."[81]

Captain Scott and the *Lapsley* were ready and waiting for the arrival of this large party.[82] There was not room for all of the Methodists and the Presbyterian missionaries also awaiting transportation upriver. The latter gladly agreed to wait in Kinshasa until the mission steamer could return to get them.[83]

Dr. D. L. Mumpower wrote enthusiastically of the assistance given to them by their brothers in Christ:

> The establishment of our church in this continent has been a matter of prayer among the Presbyterians of Luebo for over ten years. . . . In London, the same firm that acts as representative of the Presbyterian mission is also our chosen

representative. The same Mr. Robert Whyte whom Samuel
N. Lapsley speaks of in his diary with such gratitude,
welcomed us into his home, prayed with us and bade us
Godspeed on our journey. . . . On shipboard Dr. William
Morrison answered our unending questions . . . and made
out for us a short analysis of his Grammar of the Buluba
language, which has been of immense value in grasping the
principles of the Batetela language. . . .

At Stanley Pool we again fell into the hands of the
Presbyterians. Their steamboat, the *Samuel N. Lapsley*, was
awaiting us, one of the best craft on the river. It carried us
1,000 miles farther on our journey. . . . We were landed at
Luebo, the center of Presbyterian missionary work in
Central Africa. Here again the Presbyterians fell upon us,
captured us, with no resistance, and took us to their homes.

For a whole week we had the pleasure of being entertained
by this mission. . . . From their store we were supplied with
necessary articles we had failed to purchase in London.
From their dispensary we purchased medicines. From their
printing office we obtained blackboards, stationery, Batetela
hymn books and catechisms. They gave us valuable suggestions as to pay and management of workmen and cashed
our check for 5,000 francs without question. . . . They again
put us on the *Lapsley*, giving us an encouraging and
inspiring ovation as we left, and sent us on to another of
their stations, Lusambo, several hundred miles closer to our
work.[84]

On January 5, 1914, the Methodist caravan left Lusambo for
Wembo Nyama. The group consisted of ten U.S. citizens: Dr.
Lambuth and Mr. Mangum of the Methodist Board of Missions,
the six new missionaries with baby Elizabeth Mumpower, and
Rev. R. D. Bedinger of the American Presbyterian mission staff at
Lusambo. These were accompanied by thirty hammock men, two
cooks with their assistants, five personal assistants, thirty Luebo
Church members, and 148 porters, carrying 74 loads, a grand total
of 235 persons.[85]

Bishop Lambuth and Ruling Elder Mudimbi headed the caravan, next were the new missionaries, then the Luebo Christians and the porters. Mr. Mangum and Mr. Bedinger brought up the rear. Wrote Mr. Bedinger:

> It was a "sight for sore eyes," the caravan stretching for a quarter of a mile along the trail. . . . It was also interesting to see the five tents erected each evening in the villages where we spent the nights. . . . Baby Elizabeth Mumpower received the most applause and admiration![86]

A white baby was a real curiosity! Crossing over rivers on swinging vine bridges was a feat in itself for that many people.

Bob Bedinger remained at Wembo Nyama two weeks, helping with language interpretation, staking off the new concession for the mission station two miles from the chief's village and helping with all the "palavers" necessary for organizing the Methodist Church in Central Africa. Ten thousand native Christians back at Luebo had promised to be praying for these important initial events in the establishment of the new mission.[87]

The First Missionaries Sent from the Luebo Church

Ruling Elder Mudimbi was accompanied on this journey by his wife, Baba Malundolo. She, like her husband, was from the Batetela ethnic group. When she was only five years old, she had gone with her playmates down to the spring to bathe. When the children returned, they found their village deserted. A band of marauding slavers had been there! Suddenly, the children had been grabbed, tied with ropes, and led away to be sold. With her own eyes Malundolo had watched as old Chief Ngongo Lutete enclosed some of the little ones in a straw hut, then set it on fire to amuse himself with their screams. She had put her hands over her ears to shut out the terrible sounds of their agony. In Ngongo Lutete's village she had witnessed the slashing off of ears and hands, the tyrant's way of dealing with any that displeased him.[88]

Miss Maria Fearing (center, left) and Miss Lilian Thomas (center, right) maintained Luebo station's home for girls redeemed by missionaries from slavery. Standing at Miss Fearing's right is Malundolo who became wife of Elder Mudimbi. Courtesy— Department of History, PCUSA, Montreat, North Carolina.

She had been redeemed by Dr. and Mrs. Snyder, Luebo missionaries, and reared in the Girls' Home by Miss Maria Fearing. Mudimbi selected her as his wife because of their common origin and because of her beauty and keen intellect. She was one of Dr. Morrison's most reliable assistants in his compiling of the Tshiluba dictionary.[89]

Together with twenty-eight other Luebo Christians, this couple formed the nucleus of the new church at Wembo Nyama. Only two weeks after the Methodist mission was founded, a church was organized and evangelistic work begun. Such was the caliber of the Luebo Christians who gladly assumed the Methodist "label." Dr. Mumpower rejoiced: "The relationship of these two missions must fill with joy the great heart of the Lord Jesus, who prayed 'that they all may be one.'"[90]

The *Lapsley* and the Swedish Baptist Mission

On one of Captain McKinnon's upriver trips, a lad in a small dugout canoe paddled frantically out from the shore as the *Lapsley* passed the village of Bendela on the banks of the Kasai River.[91] Thinking that the boy was trying to pass in front of the steamer, McKinnon blew several sharp blasts on the whistle to make him turn around. Somehow the boy managed to pull alongside the moving vessel, grab one of the brace rods supporting the upper deck, kick his canoe out into the river, and pull himself aboard. He was seized immediately by the ship's sentry and taken to the captain. When asked why on earth he had done such a foolish, dangerous thing, he replied:

> Kapitene, my elder brother went to Luebo on the Steamer of God with Captain Scott several years ago. He learned to read books and write and about your God of Love. He told me I could come on this steamer too, and that you would take me to Luebo, let me go to school and learn what my brother learned. Then, I want to come back and help my brother teach our people the Palaver of God.

With the captain's approval, the lad was taken to the lower deck and given a place to sleep among the woodcutters. At Luebo, he became one of Dr. Motte Martin's boarding students, remaining there until he had finished the course of training offered by the American Presbyterian Congo Mission. Then the *Lapsley* took him back downriver to his home village, where he joined his elder brother in teaching, using the Tshiluba language and school text-books printed at Luebo.[92]

In 1916, a group of eight Swedish Baptist missionaries, who had been trained for two years by the Mennonites at Djoka Punda, began searching for their own mission site. They had learned to speak Tshiluba and were supplied with all the Luebo teaching materials in that language. Floating in dugout canoes down the Kasai River with their camping outfits, they stopped many times to check out possible sites for a mission station, but so far none had met all their requirements. Above all, they were hampered by not knowing the local Bomba dialect.

Finally, they came to Bendela. Two young Bomba tribesmen trained at Luebo came racing down to the shore and to their amazement welcomed them in Tshiluba, which they could understand. "Surely, *you* are the missionaries we have been praying for, to teach our people. Praise God!" they shouted.

The searchers for a new mission site set up camp there, delighted to be able to communicate immediately with the eager villagers through two such willing interpreters. Amazingly, investigation of the surroundings revealed that this site met with all their specifications. A concession was soon granted and construction began at the new location. By 1920 the Swedish Baptist mission had seven thriving stations in that area. Two small, unexpected *Lapsley* passengers had prepared the way for a great work![93]

The *Lapsley* Acquires a Belgian Engineer Captain
1913–1925

Joseph Toussaint Daumery was born at Bornesse, Belgium, in 1881. He was a graduate of the Technical School of Liege; from 1898 to 1903 he majored there in mechanics, electronics, chemistry, and architecture.[94] He served as a missionary of the *Eglise Chretienne Missionaire Belge* in French Equatorial Africa until the 1914 outbreak of World War I in Europe, which forced the indefinite closure of his mission. Searching for guidance as to his future work, Daumery went to Brazzaville and across Stanley Pool to Kinshasa. His intention was to make the upriver journey to Tshofa to visit the concession for a mission station recently granted to his church by Belgian Congo authorities; as yet, no work had been begun there. Captain Scott accepted him as a passenger and he made the journey as far as Luebo with Bishop Lambuth and his party.[95]

Luebo missionaries soon recognized the unique practical skills of their Belgian Protestant guest. He was urged to remain at Luebo and take over the operation of the J. Leighton Wilson Press, which he did in a most acceptable manner.[96] This was for Daumery the beginning of fifteen years of faithful, efficient service with the American Presbyterian Congo Mission.

In April 1915, Captain McKinnon took Daumery with him on the *Lapsley* to Kinshasa to bring up the machinery for a new sawmill which had been shipped to the mission from the United States. A large gift had been donated for the erection of the McKowen Memorial Hospital at Luebo. The sawmill was badly needed for cutting lumber for that important new structure, as well as other permanent buildings going up at Luebo. Up until then, boards had been laboriously handsawn by sawyers working over a pit.

With the help of a small crane graciously made available by the Kinshasa railroad stationmaster, the two-ton boiler, the heaviest piece of the new sawmill, was unloaded from the flatcar. The rest of the dismounted machinery was divided into loads that were carried to the steamer on long poles by four to six men. Six heavy planks were laid down to form a track on which the boiler was moved to the beach by sheer manpower, some thirty men pulling with ropes while others pushed. It was then pulled onto the *Lapsley* by the anchor cable attached to the steamer's winch. McKinnon described the problem he and Daumery and the crew faced:

> We had to take out the stairway leading to the upper deck in order to find space long enough for the boiler. The square firebox was riveted onto one end of the boiler to keep it from rolling off. We had to anchor it carefully so that it would remain in the center of the steamer and not slip to one side or the other. . . . This made the load top-heavy, but we managed to get up to Luebo without serious trouble.[97]

In July 1915, Captain Scott left the *Lapsley*, carefully guarded, safely anchored in deep water at Basongo, the junction of the Kasai and Sankuru Rivers. He and his wife resigned at that time for health reasons and left for good. Alternate Captain and Mrs. McKinnon also left then on regular furlough. The *Lapsley* was left without a captain.[98]

The November 1915 issue of the *Kasai Herald* begins with an apology for its late appearance that month, caused by "the absence of Mr. Daumery, who has charge of the printing department." But it goes right on in the following article to rejoice over the arrival of the *Lapsley* with fifteen missionaries aboard—the largest number ever brought up from Kinshasa by the mission steamer. "We are profoundly thankful to our Heavenly Father for the splendid voyage which has been made by our new Captain, Mr. Daumery! Both passengers and crew united in their praise of him and the remarkable success of his first command. Perhaps one reason for that success was the presence on board of one well-educated young lady—Mlle Nelly Balty, his fiancée! Soon after her arrival she became Mrs. Daumery."[99]

The *Lapsley* Endures a "Rocky" Experience

When the McKinnons returned from home leave in 1916, Captain Daumery and the *Lapsley* were waiting at Kinshasa. McKinnon recorded:

> We began our journey on October 28th. We had a very good trip all the way until we were in sight of the native village of Luebo, where the steamer ran onto the edge of a big sand bar. This pushed us off course and onto the rocks at the other side of the river. After several attempts to back the steamer off the rocks, we discovered that one of the jagged boulders had broken a hole in the front plate of the boat and water was pouring in. We sent the passengers ashore in the lifeboat while Mr. Daumery and I helped the native crew bail out the water and make a temporary patch for the broken place. We finally succeeded in getting the hole stopped by means of wooden blocks driven into the hold and bracing them with wedges between the blocks and under the surface of the floor of the upper deck. We finally pulled up to the mission beach on November 15th.

> After unloading the steamer we were able to jack up the
> front part of the boat so that the broken plate was above the
> water level. By this means we were able to patch the hole
> more securely so as to make it safe for the trip down to Dima
> for permanent repairs.[100]

Two weeks later word was received that the Cranes, Vinsons,
and Kellersbergers would be arriving from Matadi the first week
of December. Because of baby Raymond Daumery's serious illness,
Alternate Captain McKinnon made the trip down to Kinshasa. The
temporary repairs that the two captains had made on the *Lapsley*
were holding so well that a stop was made at Dima only long
enough to arrange for permanent repairs to be made on return.[101]

As planned, the mission steamer stopped at Dima on the way
back upriver for that necessary welding job to be done on the front
plate. Fortunately, a tiny Company Kasai auxiliary boat was
leaving that same day for Luebo. The *Lapsley's* passengers made
the remainder of their journey on the *Antoinette*. On Christmas

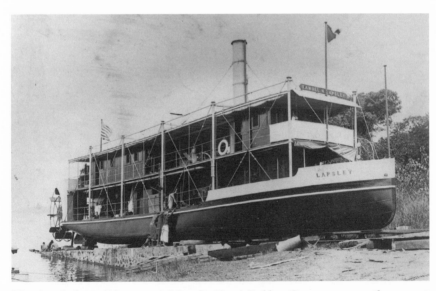

*The dry docks at Dima, owned by the Kasai Rubber Company, were the nearest
facility to Luebo where the* Lapsley *could be regularly overhauled and painted.
Courtesy—Department of History, PCUSA, Montreat, North Carolina.*

A line of crewmen, standing in shallow water covering a sandbar, attempt to dislodge the Lapsley *by pulling on ropes while the stern-wheel rotates. Courtesy— Department of History, PCUSA, Montreat, North Carolina.*

Day 1916, the three couples, seated on the small deck, sang old familiar Christmas carols to the strange accompaniment of the rhythmic swishing of the miniature paddle wheel and the unexpected splash of crocodiles and hippos, startled from their sunning spots on the sandbanks by the passing steamer. The arrival of the missionaries at Luebo a few days later was not the same as it would have been had they been aboard the *Lapsley*. When the large crowd of Christians waiting at the landing sang a joyous hymn of welcome, the crew of the Belgian steamer had no idea that a hymn of response was expected from *them*![102]

The damaged steel plate on the *Lapsley's* bow was removed at Dima and a new plate riveted on. The mission steamer returned to Luebo on January 1, 1917, in its usual prime condition, with no evidence of the harrowing "rocky" experience.[103]

Captain Daumery and the *Lapsley* as Goodwill Ambassadors

Four round-trip journeys were made by the *Lapsley* during the 1917 rainy season. On one of these journeys the steamer was again hauled out of the water at Dima, headquarters of the Kasai Rubber Company. A thorough overhauling and a fresh coat of paint made the vessel ready again for its continued service to the mission. Surprisingly, for this much-needed work, the Kasai Rubber Company rendered no bill. It claimed a grateful indebtedness to the mission's medical staff for looking after the health of its agents at Luebo and Lusambo. How the relationship had changed between the mission and the rubber company from the time of its bitter legal action against Sheppard and Morrison in 1909 at Kinshasa![104]

Part of the task of being a *Lapsley* captain was being responsible for observing the colonial government laws controlling river travel, the treatment of crew members, and care of steamer passengers. Individual "Travel Permits" (*Attestations d'Immatriculation*), for instance, were required to be carried at all times by both crew and passengers.[105]

Handling such legal aspects of being captain of the mission steamer presented no problem to Daumery, a native Belgian. His nationality and his fluent use of his native French were tremendous assets. He was respected for his integrity and graciousness by both Belgians and Congolese alike up and down the rivers whose waters the *Lapsley* plied.

Above all, Captain Daumery was a real Protestant Christian, something rare in Catholic Belgium, where Protestantism had been virtually wiped out by the Spanish Inquisition which began in 1566. It is estimated that one hundred thousand Protestant believers were killed during that terrible time. In 1914, when Daumery transferred his missionary service to the American Presbyterian Congo Mission, the *Eglise Chretienne Missionaire Belge*, of which he was a member, had only twelve thousand registered members and thirty pastors. Previously, there had been some six hundred pastors ministering in Belgium. Wherever Captain Daumery went, he never failed to give a winsome witness to his strong, simple faith. The Christian ministry of the *Samuel N. Lapsley* was greatly enhanced by this fine Belgian Protestant captain.[106]

The *Lapsley* Responds to a Medical Emergency

Passengers on board the mission steamer in November 1919 were Dr. and Mrs. Eugene Kellersberger and their little daughter, Winifred. Dr. Kellersberger graphically described what occurred on November 21 on the downriver trip, captained by Daumery:

> Along the winding banks of the Kasai River there are scattered here and there small trading posts far removed from other white men, and in case of need, far from help. Some are traders, others are hunters of big game, others, planters. They may be almost any nationality—Belgian, French, English, Portuguese, Italian, Swiss or Greek! They are usually men seeking wealth, or dissatisfied, chafing spirits seeking relief from the restraints of civilization. Some have left their countries because of an unsavory past. As a rule morals and religion are unimportant to such men, and they do not usually take the best themselves. They dare the climate, the powerful sun and the crafty mosquito and laugh at warnings. As a consequence, the sad end of many a mother's son far away from home has been a bed of burning fever, a wild delirium and a lonely, forgotten grave in some deserted spot of Africa's high grass.

> The *Lapsley* was coming rapidly downriver around a great bend one sunny afternoon, with a far-reaching stretch of glassy water before her, when the call came. A white flag was up at the next trading post. Someone was asking us to stop at this lonely spot for some reason. With one long whistle we answered, "We are coming!" Slowly swinging around and tying up at the grassy bank, we were handed the following message, "Is there a doctor on board? There is a man here very sick with blackwater fever."

> There he lay, a fine big physical specimen, on a poor bed in the darkened room of a mud and grass house. Immediately the attention was arrested by the ominous, penetrating mouse-like odor of a man sick with the viper of all tropical diseases, the dreaded blackwater fever. The telltale white

eyegrounds, the pale nails, the sallow yellow-brown skin, the rapid pulse and labored respiration, the burning fever, the powerful retching and vomiting, all of these together gave the picture of a dangerously sick man. There he lay, now restless, now lucid, now talking disconnectedly or dropping into a suspicious, stuporous sleep.

Day and night for three days the fearful struggle went on in his powerful body, while the *Lapsley*, the "steamer of God," waited patiently. Then Monday night at eight o'clock, after a short struggle, this troubled soul left its earthly house and the once powerful, tall, proud body lay there utterly broken. Death is the great revealer of men's hearts and thoughts. His poor wife—but no! she said, trembling, that she wasn't his wife, only living with him. She had cried as some of us had prayed and talked with him during his lucid moments, begging him to accept the Only One Who can forgive sins and give peace.

The very same day that he died, letters and pictures came from a dear old mother and a faithful brother in far off Belgium, pleading with him to write. He never saw those pictures or letters but pictures of his lonely grave on the banks of the Kasai, of his house on the hill were taken and are being sent to his old mother, with the comforting news that he was ministered to until the last breath with loving hands and laid gently in the ground. The woman who lived with him cried out to us as we left, "I never thought that there were any people in the Congo that would do for us what you have done! God bless you!"[107]

The 1922 General Conference of Protestant Missions at Bolenge

By 1918, the General Conference of Protestant Missions, born of necessity for union during the dark days of the old Congo Free State, had grown to a large active organization. Dr. William McCutchan Morrison was its elected head when the American

Presbyterian Congo Mission hosted the February 1918 meeting at Luebo. He died on March 14, 1918, shortly after its closing.

The Reverend Chal Vinson recalled:

> Dr. Morrison presided over the sessions of the Conference in the most impartial and tactful manner. . . . Only on one occasion did the discussion begin to strike fire. Dr. Morrison very calmly stopped the proceedings for a word of prayer and asked the two contending brethren to lead in that prayer. It was a master stroke, for a smile began to break over their faces and when the prayers were ended, the discussion ceased. Dr. Morrison had completely won the hearts of all those present at the Conference, which fact was evidenced when he was again unanimously chosen to be their President during the next four years.[108]

In October 1922, it was time for the quadrennial meeting of the organization. Rev. Robert D. Bedinger and Mr. Frank J. Gilliam were the American Presbyterian Congo Mission delegates. Mr. Bedinger's account of that meeting highlights the efficient, willing services of Captain and Mrs. Daumery, who hosted such a large number of passengers, and the faithful, trustworthy *Lapsley*:

> In October we had the privilege of attending the *General Conference of Protestant Missionaries in the Belgian Congo*. This Conference was held at Bolenge on the Congo River, an American Mission of the Disciples of Christ. They had planned to entertain one hundred delegates and were not disappointed for we all appeared, with three over for good measure! Our own Mission Boat, the *Lapsley*, left Lusambo with Captain Daumery in charge; the passengers were Dr. and Mrs. Mumpower, of our sister Southern Methodist Mission, and the three Bedingers. When we reached the Kasai River we were joined by Mr. Gilliam of our Mission and Mr. Everett of the Northern Methodist Mission. As we proceeded up the Congo River, missionaries of other denominations and other nationalities came on board till we numbered seventeen in all. Needless to say, we had a goodly number of deck passengers towards the end of the journey.

On our arrival we were welcomed with true American enthusiasm and pleasure. . . . Delegates were requested to bring their camp cots. Some of them were housed in a new brick industrial building, while others of us slept on the three mission steamers. We assembled in another large brick building for meals. . . .

I'll never forget our communion service at Bolenge when English, Swedes, Belgians and Americans representing twelve denominations, gathered around the Lord's Table. I doubt if there was a dry eye in the congregation as our leader read the names of those who had been called to Higher Service since the last meeting of the Conference at Luebo in 1918. Our own Dr. Morrison, Ex-President of this Conference, was the first name to be read. . . . Our cooperative work will not be in the least confusing to the native believers as we never teach them denominational differences.

As the *Lapsley* pulled out from the Bolenge beach the friends on board as well as on shore joined in singing, "Blest be the tie that binds." Our return journey started with sixteen passengers on board and we gradually lost all of them save those returning to Luebo for our own Annual Mission Meeting.[109]

Sandbanks Continue To Plague the *Lapsley*

Throughout 1923 and 1924 Captain Daumery continued to take the *Lapsley* on as many trips as necessary during the rainy season. The heavy rains usually began the last week in August, increasing in number and intensity as September passed. The Plumer Smith family, however, was scheduled to board the Belgian ocean liner at Matadi for home leave the last week of that month. The water level was still dry-season-low, but the trip from Lusambo to Kinshasa had to be made.

On September 5, 1923, Plumer Smith described in his inimitable style the events of this difficult downriver journey:

Yesterday at 4 p.m. we got stuck on a sandbank. We were stuck there for 22 hours. The fun was ours. The work and worry belonged to Captain Daumery. The system is to take the anchor off into deep water, some 100 yards away and drop it. Then, by pulling with the winch to wind up the cable, the *Lapsley* is pulled out into deep water. Quite easy? But the *Lapsley* weighs 80 tons and the cargo, 20 and the firewood, 5! The men get tired of turning the winch crank. Captain Daumery was up all night for fear the boat might in some way get off the sandbank and begin to drift downstream. During the night, half the wood for the boiler was taken ashore in a small boat.

One man got his garb caught in the cogs of the winch. It was turned into *corduroy*! No harm done! We finally got into deep water. Another two hours was required for the crew to eat and reload the wood. . . .

At Dima, the headquarters of the Company Kasai, we picked up Rev. and Mrs. McKinnon and the John Morrisons (also on their way to Matadi), who had come on another boat from Luebo.[110]

Daumery Is Relieved of the Captaincy

The responsibility for operating the *Lapsley* increased in complexity as the years passed. In 1920 the Daumerys were moved from Luebo to Lusambo, the transport station, because of the growing volume of business transactions between the Presbyterian and Methodist Missions. Mr. Higgins, a joint agent for both missions secured by Bishop Lambuth, was handling transport problems at Lusambo in a very businesslike manner, but the amount of paperwork and red tape necessary for billing the missions and securing the necessary licenses and travel permits was becoming overwhelming.

The Methodists now had their own small steamer, the thirty-five-horsepower *Texas*, a gift of the Epworth Leagues of Texas. The Lusambo mission "fleet" was growing.[111]

Other changes which made the captaincy more difficult were
the automobiles now in use on the stations, necessitating special
trips to and from Kinshasa for carrying only drums of gasoline.
The *Lapsley* was also sometimes having to carry passengers other
than missionaries and cargo for traders. For these reasons and
more, Captain Daumery felt that his captaincy should be termi-
nated, which it was by mission action on October 13, 1925.[112]

Whenever the *Lapsley* was inactive during dry seasons at
Luebo, the Daumerys were always busy teaching in the Luebo
schools, something they thoroughly enjoyed. Their native French
was a tremendous asset to the students. So, after leaving the
captaincy, the couple requested the mission allow them to teach
full time, and that is what they did until their resignation for
health reasons in April 1929. As the captain and as the ship's
hostess of the *Lapsley* and as teachers, this gifted couple made a
remarkable contribution to the work of the American Presbyterian
Congo Mission.[113]

Rev. S. H. Wilds—The Dentist Captain
1923–1929

The Reverend Samuel Hugh Wilds was a missionary of the
American Presbyterian Congo Mission from 1912 to 1957. Born in
Georgetown, South Carolina, he attended the University of South
Carolina for two years and then completed his college education at
Davidson College in North Carolina. He received further training
at Hyatt Park Institute and Columbia Theological Seminary, after
which he was ordained to the ministry of the Presbyterian Church,
U.S.[114]

During his first term on the field, working as an evangelistic
missionary, he became keenly aware of the need of the mission for
on-the-field dental care, the nearest dentist being 950 miles away
in Brazzaville. On each of his home leaves, Mr. Wilds was given
permission to study dentistry. He acquired the basic equipment
necessary for taking care of the primary emergency dental needs of
his fellow missionaries. In his later years on the field he had a large

truck fitted with a chair and all his equipment. Each year he made regular rounds to the Presbyterian and Methodist mission stations to take care of routine dental work.

In addition to his regular duties as a minister and a dentist, Wilds was also captain and alternate captain of the *Lapsley*. From 1923 to 1929, he was very active in this third capacity, proving himself as capable at the ship's wheel as he was with his Bible or dental drill. Even though he accumulated several years of experience in dental schools in the United States, he was never officially licensed to practice dentistry there. Mr. Wilds's dental functions were limited entirely to his Congo missionary colleagues, their wives and children, and the many Congolese who requested his services. Belgian officials and Portuguese traders were also relieved of many a toothache by his caring services. His was truly a very special three-fold ministry.[115]

The *Lapsley* Serves as a Mortuary

The Reverend Hershey Longenecker recorded one of the more unusual *Lapsley* experiences that occurred in 1926 during Wilds's captaincy:

> As we were passing the little post of a Danish trader on the Kasai River, he signaled to our captain to come to shore. So, Captain Wilds anchored near his place. The trader came aboard and explained that he lived alone with his native help. The day before, a Belgian had been hunting upstream. He wounded a hippo, which then attacked and destroyed his canoe, and killed the hunter. The employees of this Belgian carried their master's corpse to the Danish trader's post, then ran away, leaving the problem of burial to him. But his own workmen were superstitious, and would not lift a hand to help him. He could not bury the man alone. Would Captain Wilds kindly lend him the steamer's crew for the interment? So, our journey was interrupted. A rude coffin was quickly made, and neatly covered with cloth. It was draped in a Belgian flag, and one of the missionaries

conducted a funeral service. As a comfort to the family of the deceased in Belgium, I took a photograph of the coffin and grave, and sent it through a local official to the man's parents. In due time I received a nice letter of appreciation.[116]

The *Lapsley* Confronts Lediba Pass

By 1928 the American Presbyterian Congo Mission had six widely scattered stations: Luebo (1891), Mutoto (1912), Lusambo (1913), Bulape (1915), Bibanga (1917), and Lubondai (1925). Full-time overseas missionaries numbered 74. There were 486 mission outposts and a Church membership of 20,576. The mission school system had 1,118 native teachers, 20,061 day-school students and 641 second-degree students. There were 1,132 older boys and girls in mission boarding homes. Five mission hospitals were handling a maximum number of patients, requiring large supplies of drugs and equipment. The Carson Industrial School was turning out trained carpenters and masons. The J. Leighton Wilson Press was in full operation, supplying textbooks for the schools, medical forms for the hospitals, and all the printed matter used in the outstations and churches for instruction in the Christian faith.[117]

Essential cargo needed for such a growing work far exceeded the capacity of the *Lapsley's* hold. It had become necessary for heavily loaded barges of supplies and equipment to be towed upriver on special cargo trips.

The three greatest navigational danger points along the usual route taken by the *Lapsley* up the lower Zaire and Kasai Rivers were Kwamouth, the junction of the two rivers, and the Swinburne and Lediba Passes. At each of these, steamer wrecks had occurred with loss of life. The first *Lapsley* and other vessels capsized at Kwamouth because of the tremendous whirlpools created by the differing water levels of the Zaire and the Kasai.

The *Roi des Belges*, with much mission mail aboard, was wrecked in 1906 on the huge, menacing rock formations of Swinburne Pass. The pass had been named for King Leopold's explorer who turned back at this point, convinced that the Kasai was not navigable beyond it.[118]

Lediba Pass is most treacherous because of extremely powerful currents, particularly during the dry season months of June and July. There the Kasai, shallow and broad, suddenly narrows into a constricted channel, very difficult to navigate.[119]

In July 1927, the Methodist mission steamer *Texas* struggled for an hour, making no headway whatsoever through Lediba Pass. Suddenly it was twisted around and around, then catapulted back downriver. Passengers and crew were marooned on a sandbank for five days, waiting for higher water.[120]

In July 1929, the *Lapsley*, pulling two heavily loaded barges, approached Lediba Pass. Even with her powerful engines, the mission steamer failed to get through the pass. Turning back downriver and stopping in a safe place, passengers and crew joined in a prayer service, asking for guidance and protection. The decision was made to attempt to pull the barges through, one at a time. The larger of the barges was tied securely to a bank, life jackets were donned by all aboard and a second attempt was made, towing only one barge. This time, the *Lapsley* succeeded, but not without terrifying moments when it seemed as if the maelstrom would win! In quiet waters above the pass, a grateful praise service was held.

Then, down through the violent trough the *Lapsley* went to get the second, larger barge. Once again the sturdy stern-wheeler, its boiler roaring with flames, mustered all its engine powers and succeeded. Again, safely through, engines were stopped and a praise service held, thanking God for practical, gracious guidance, and miraculous protection of both life and property.[121]

Captain Wilds later commented about this experience:

> Captain Vass gave the Scottish shipbuilding company a real understanding of what kind of steamer was needed, one with really powerful engines, able to combat the terrible currents of the tropical river system. The *Lapsley* always behaved itself so well in these treacherous currents, just because of those unusually powerful engines. . . . Its railroad boiler could supply plenty of steam in an emergency. Whenever there was need for emergency power, the *Lapsley* could always produce it.

At Lediba Pass the mission steamer once again proved itself equal to the river.[122]

The Stern-wheeler Was "Home, Sweet Home"

The hostess of the *Lapsley* was usually the captain's wife. It was her duty to welcome passengers aboard and escort them to their assigned cabins, always scrupulously cleaned and supplied with freshly washed bed and bath linens.

She also planned all meals; the tables sometimes had as many as twenty place settings. She oversaw the preparation of food in the ship's galley and directed the serving of it. Purchase of chickens, ducks, eggs, vegetables, and tropical fruits were made at native markets along the riverbanks. Staples, such as flour and sugar, had to be purchased in the Kinshasa stores. With a school-age child aboard, she also had to make time for teaching. The captains' wives were busy, busy ladies!

Lucille Keller Wilds (Mrs. S. H. Wilds) was a lovely, auburn-haired Virginia girl, particularly gifted in the arts of homemaking and entertainment. During one of the mission's "Fun Night Parties," a regular part of the annual mission meetings, "Mission Superlatives" were selected. Mrs. Wilds was given the prize for being "The Salad Lady." Her famous, mouthwatering meals always included a dainty, delectable salad of some sort!

In November 1924, Rev. Plumer Smith wrote in a letter to friends: "Rev. S. H. Wilds is a good Captain and Mrs. Wilds is a good hostess. Anne, aged three, is a good playmate for our children. Our only fear is of GOUT!" That was his way of saying that all the meals Mrs. Wilds served were most plentiful and delicious.[123]

Of all the children of the mission, Anne Wilds (Now Mrs. David McLean) spent the most time aboard the *Lapsley*. For six years (1923–1929), her father, Captain S. H. Wilds, was on call at anytime for river trips. Anne's childhood memories are truly fascinating and unique:

Man-eating crocodiles such as this one are frequently encountered in the rivers of Central Africa. Courtesy—Department of History, PCUSA, Montreat, North Carolina.

I have many happy memories of my childhood in the Belgian Congo, but I think my favorites are those of the years I spent living on the *Lapsley* as the Captain's daughter. We traveled up and down the rivers, carrying large barges of supplies for the Mission, missionaries going on furlough or returning to the field, as well as Belgian, Portuguese and English passengers.

I remember going to sleep at night to a full chorus of millions of river frogs and noisy grunts of hippos nearby. I learned to skate and jump rope on that upper deck.

Whenever the *Lapsley* was in dry dock at Kinshasa, we would live as much as a month at the Union Mission House. That wide upstairs porch overlooking Stanley Pool was a wonderful classroom.

Sometimes my dad would shoot crocodiles sunning themselves on sandbanks. The crew was always delighted at the prospect of a feast. Once Dad shot a huge, man-eating type.

It was dragged onto the lower deck of the steamer, where it stretched completely across it, from one side to the other.

Someone suggested that my mother and I climb on his back and have our picture taken! About five minutes after we got off of its back, the croc started slowly crawling off the boat. Some of the crew members quickly finished it off.[124]

Captain J. F. Watt—The Bridegroom Captain
1925–1930

The last American Presbyterian Congo Mission captain the *Lapsley* had was John Franklin Watt, usually called "Franklin." He was born in Milwaukee, Wisconsin, but moved to Charleston, West Virginia, at an early age. Dr. Frank Brown of the Bream Memorial Presbyterian Church, his beloved spiritual mentor, guided his life into the direction of the mission field. He received training for work as an industrial missionary at Moody Bible Institute and the Carnegie Technology Institute. He arrived at Luebo to take up his work in August 1925.

His wife, Georgia McKay Watt, was born in Macon, Georgia, but Thomasville was her home from early childhood. She was a graduate of Georgia State College for Women and the Assembly's Training School in Richmond, Virginia. In 1921 she was appointed to the American Presbyterian Congo Mission as an education missionary.[125]

A "match made in heaven" became an earthly reality when a party of six American Presbyterian Congo missionaries sailed from New York for Belgium and the Congo on the SS *Pittsburgh*, July 16, 1925. Franklin, the new appointee, and Georgia, returning to the field from her first furlough, were among them. The trans-Atlantic voyage and the two-week-long voyage from Antwerp to Matadi gave plenty of opportunity for getting really acquainted and "falling in love."[126]

To the delight of Luebo Christians, the couple was married in the big Luebo church on July 9, 1926. Their honeymoon was one

week at Bulape Lake. From there they went to their first assignment—the captaincy of the *Lapsley*!

From her new floating home, Georgia wrote to her supporting
churches in the United States in November 1926:

> The *Lapsley* has been running now for 21 years and is still in
> such good condition that several offers have been made for
> her by commercial enterprises. But the day has not yet come
> when transport by other boats is practicable. She is no
> longer the fastest boat on the river for some of the newer
> vessels that ply up the main Congo look like ocean liners by
> the side of her and carry as many as forty passengers, where
> the *Lapsley* can carry only six comfortably. She formerly had
> a capacity of forty-five tons, but that has been decreased by
> the placing of iron tripledecker beds to accommodate the
> crew and native passengers. Now, with her new twenty-ton
> barge she can carry fifty tons. . . . Coming down on this trip
> we brought rubber, palm-kernels and rice as cargo; going
> up we have gasoline and other petroleum products,
> building materials such as metal roofing, cement, etc., salt
> and foodstuffs. My part is acting as housekeeper and
> hostess. Somebody rather appropriately dubbed me the
> "Stewardess."[127]

> Keeping enough boiled drinking water for a crowd is a job
> in itself. Our evening meal is served at a big table on the
> deck under a huge mosquito net, because of the multitude
> of flying insects. When our first child, Margot, arrived, the
> small Captain's cabin was a bit crowded, with a baby bed in
> addition to our folding beds and the big desk. She learned
> to walk holding onto the deck railings.[128]

Franklin's only previous experience on a riverboat had been as
a cabin boy on the Kanawha River in West Virginia. In an article he
wrote for the *Presbyterian Survey* in 1928, he showed how well he
had adapted to his work as captain:

> In the early days it was necessary to carry a crew of about
> fifty, which included those who cut and load firewood. The

Porters tie sturdy carrying poles to boxes of Lapsley *freight. Four carriers were often needed for the heavier boxes carried up Luebo hill. Courtesy—Department of History, PCUSA, Montreat, North Carolina.*

boat would tie up at three or four o'clock in the afternoon for it required the whole night to finish this work. Today the crew is reduced to thirty-five men, as there are now government wood posts along the river where wood, already cut to size, may be bought. The price varies from 50 to $2.50 a cord, the average being $1.50. The daily consumption is about eleven cords.

We try to get away by five o'clock in the morning. It is long journey to the post at which we wish to spend the night, but if all goes well, we reach the post just as darkness falls. One hears much of the beautiful trip up the Hudson. I've often wondered if the trip up the Congo channel isn't just as pretty. It is beautiful but rather dangerous, especially in case of storms, for sometimes it is difficult to find a place to tie-up where the boat will not strike rocks. The storms are *very* bad!

You would be surprised, no doubt, to see the steamer unable to pass a given point for perhaps ten or fifteen minutes, even though the steam gauge shows a full head of steam and the throttle is wide open on the engines. After weaving back and forth for sometime, the *Lapsley* passes through what is equal to a veritable mill-race. It requires very careful maneuvering of the boat in entering these strong currents, as they shoot around the rock-bound points of land, else we may be capsized.

Truly, the *Lapsley* has been of untold value during her many years of service. Those who gave their pennies, nickels and dimes to her purchase should feel very thankful for the opportunity that was theirs. . . . Two years ago, a man visited the Congo, and great was his pride when, after all these years, he had the privilege of boarding the *Lapsley*. As a boy in Sunday School, he had given a nickel, when funds were being raised to replace the first *Lapsley*![129]

Substitute Captains Take the Wheel

Over the years, several other American Presbyterian Congo Mission workers substituted for the regular captains or their alternates when these were for some reason unavailable. Usually the emergency was met by not more than one or two trips.

Thomas J. Arnold, the mission treasurer, filled in for awhile in 1913 when Captain and Mrs. Scott had to leave on emergency furlough because of illness.[130]

Edward H. Dowsett, a trained engineer from London, arrived in 1913 to replace Scott. He had been on the field only a few months when he was forced to return to England for health reasons in the fall of 1914. Such was the toll of tropical diseases![131]

A trip made by the *Lapsley* with Rev. Motte Martin as substitute captain is well-documented by Louise Crane. She was aboard with her parents and recalls this incident vividly:

The *Lapsley* always tied up at a wood post before dark, but one day we tied up unusually early because of a brewing storm. As we neared the shore, two crewmen jumped into the river to carry the ship's cable to the bank, where they would fasten it to a sturdy tree. Just as they hit the water, two huge crocodiles jumped in from the opposite bank. The water was a churning mass of human legs and crocodile tails. One of the men cried out, "It caught me! I'm dying!" Captain Martin, an expert shot, aimed his rifle and hit one of the crocodiles. Suddenly, all was still. The two men struggled ashore unharmed, but just as they pulled out of the water, a third crocodile jumped in from the bank beside them. Miraculously, the terrified men made it back to the ship safely. Adventures like this were rather common on the *Lapsley*.[132]

William J. Anderson was another interim *Lapsley* captain pressed into service:

Since I came to the Congo six months ago, I have done more different things than I ever did in six years back home. First, I was transport manager at Lusambo . . . then, station treasurer. Then I became director of the workline, superintendent of repairs and upkeep, manufacturer of new furniture, landscape gardener, student of Tshiluba, and station barber, architect, contractor, builder, brick manufacturer and surveyor. On top of it all, I was the humble servant of Mrs. Anderson!

Now I have added to the above titles "Captain of the *S.S. Lapsley*!" . . . I have to get up before four in the morning to get the firemen started. They are not in the least afraid of the boiler; after long months of training they still persist in firing the cold boiler as hard as they can fire it. One morning, when I had gone back to bed and dozed off, I was aroused by the safety valve popping off at 150 pounds pressure just one hour after the fire had been started in the cold boiler! But we are still here and all is well!

When steam is nearly up, I ring the ship's bell for morning prayers. We meet at the foot of the steps on the lower deck and have a Bible reading, hymn and a prayer by one of the crewmen, all in the dark, save for one small lantern to read by. Then things move quickly. The first whistle is blown as soon as the morning light is bright enough to see the sand-banks; the second whistle follows closely. Then the gangplank is drawn, we cast off and we are on our day's journey before six.

From then on, the Captain scarcely leaves the bridge. He eats his meals there, and he sits right by the control, looking out for sand, snags, etc. We have two good African wheelmen who can decipher the course wonderfully well. And two other crewmen are sitting up near the bow, constantly taking soundings. Right now the river is high so we have practically no trouble with sand. Of course, we have to wind back and forth from one bank to another to follow the channel. . . . In all, this trip will take at last three weeks.

But all the time I am here, my work back at Lusambo is dragging. I had just completed the excavation for a permanent kiln to burn bricks, when I was called to take the *Lapsley*! When I return, I suppose the rains will have washed all the sand and dirt back into the excavation again! But that is the way things go when there are so few men for the work.[133]

Carroll Stegall was another industrial missionary who had to drop his work for a short-term captaincy of the *Lapsley*. The Stegall's daughter, always called by her Tshiluba nickname, "Sanky," has clear memories of the crocodiles sunning on river-banks and the monstrous heads of hippos suddenly submerging. She remembers the "hot, humid nights, trying to sleep in the tiny cabin, under the mosquito net."

She also recalls that her dad loved to play practical jokes. Secretly, he had a monkey cooked in the ship's galley and served at the dinner table, unknown to the new missionaries. "After they had tasted the delicacy and complimented the chef, they found out what they were eating," says Sanky. "You can imagine the consternation that followed!" Hearing this story, Frank McElroy Jr. commented, "My parents (Jane and Frank McElroy Sr.) were 'treated' to this experience!"

Sanky's most vivid memory is a sad, unsolved mystery. One night her father tied up the *Lapsley* for the night at a wood post where a Belgian family lived. The Stegalls and their only passenger, a Belgian boy going home for vacation, were invited to dinner. The missionary family gladly accepted the invitation, but the boy, who was shy, refused to go with them. Reluctantly, the Stegalls walked up the hill, leaving the boy aboard the steamer with the crew.

When they returned the lad was nowhere to be found. Crewmen reported that he was last seen, sitting on the edge of the lower deck with his feet dangling in the water. It could only be assumed that a crocodile had pulled him under, as he was never seen again.[134]

"Mish Kids" Cherish *Lapsley* Memories

The years that the children of the American Presbyterian Congo Mission traveled on the *Lapsley* with their parents are long gone, but memories of those river steamer journeys are for them still vividly real.

Anne Boyd Cleveland (Mrs. Henry Crane) recalls:

> . . . I remember how frightening it was as as child of four or five to stand at the top of the stairs that went from the upper deck down to the "boiler deck." I remember that roaring hot boiler, being fed log after log all day long. African freight of every description was stored there. The river was so near, only inches below deck level. It was amazing that they could keep anything on board, let alone the goats and chickens!

> I recall how strict Mother was in putting long, ribbed stockings on us at evening time to protect us from mosquitoes. Those stockings were so hot and uncomfortable, but we suffered through it.[135]

Ruth Smith Gilmer took special pride in being aboard "her father's boat." Rev. Plumer Smith had told his little daughter how

Ruth Smith and Eva King enjoy a stroll ashore, while woodmen load wood on the Lapsley *for the next day's journey. (October 1924). Courtesy—Mrs. J. B. (Ruth Smith) Gilmer.*

in 1894, as a lad of five, his Sunday school class in Westminster, South Carolina, worked to raise money for a mission river steamer in Africa. Little Plumer planted potato eyes in a field on his father's farm. When the potatoes grew, he sold them and gave a whole dollar for building the first *Lapsley*. He had a certificate to prove it! Mr. Smith also contributed to the construction of the second *Lapsley*. He laughingly said that he had come to the Belgian Congo to "ride on *his* steamer!"

Ruth smiles when she recalls playing with Anne Wilds, the captain's daughter: "She showed me how well she could shinny up the deck stanchions. I was quite impressed!"[136]

Elizabeth McKee (Mrs. Ben F. Gerding) recollects being on board the *Lapsley* on the trip captained by Franklin Watt on his way to be married to Miss Georgia McKay. Passengers kept kidding him about "speeding up" in order to get to Luebo as soon as

Rev. and Mrs. Plumer Smith oversee an early supper on the Lapsley deck for Robert and Mesu King, Anne Wilds, Eva King, and Ruth Smith. Courtesy—Mrs. J. B. (Ruth Smith) Gilmer.

possible. She also recalls the evening stops to load wood and how frighteningly close to the water the lower deck passengers traveled. Once they stopped to kill a crocodile sunning on a sand-bank to provide a feast for the "lower deck folk." She does not remember the "upper deck folk" ever having it for dinner.[137]

Many memories of Dorothy Longenecker (Mrs. Joseph Hopper) have to do with the threat of tropical insects:

> We always wore light-colored clothing and were warned to watch out for tsetse flies which might light on us. They could be recognized by wings with anvil patterns in them, folded on top of each other. These flies carry the dreaded African Sleeping Sickness, which, by God's mercy, nobody in the Longenecker family ever got. . . . One morning we were taken to look at the mass of mosquitoes trapped between the mosquito netting and wall of a lady-passenger's cabin. I don't think there was a square inch without mosquitoes.

Dorothy and her sister Alice recall that the dishes on board the steamer did not all match. Two of them were dubbed by the children, the "lucky plates." They were always excited, prior to a meal, to see who would get these plates. The sisters also recall one night that they felt very insecure. A large crocodile had been shot and put onto a barge tied to the lower deck just outside their cabin door. They were glad when it was gone.

Like Anne Wilds, the Longenecker girls enjoyed trying to climb the deck stanchions, competing to see who could shinny the highest. Another fun time was when Captain Watt took his early morning bath in a tub of river water, right next door to their cabin. Dorothy reflected:

> To amuse us little girls, he made all sorts of strange animal noises and bird whistles to amuse us and we listened with great glee. Some memories were not that happy. One day an African crew member, seeking to dip water from the river with a bucket, fell over board. We watched his head as he was carried downriver in the fast current. It looked like a football. The little boat tied to the *Lapsley* could not reach him before his head went under.[138]

Dr. John Knox Miller writes:

> In 1929 we returned from the States and traveled upriver on the *Lapsley*. I recall eating our meals on the open deck behind the Captain's quarters. On one occasion an elephant that was down at the water did not see us until we were just opposite; then it went charging off into the bush. My parents were trying at that moment to hide a quinine capsule in Alfred's porridge without success until the elephant appeared and then down it went! I also recall the daily squabbles among the children about who could look through the knothole in the rear deck to watch the paddle-wheel going around. We were not allowed on the lower deck, which swarmed with Congolese, so the knothole was our only recourse. Of course, we went aground regularly, since it was the dry season and we kids enjoyed watching the anchors being ferried out in a small boat, to allow

winching the boat off the sandbar. The evenings were also
interesting as we watched the gang of men go ashore and
hunt logs and sticks to chop up for the boiler. The flood
lights lit up the shore for hours after sunset for this
activity.[139]

The forbidden stairway leading down to the lower deck, the
lively, noisy stir and smells of everyday village life just below;
the voracious maw of the roaring boiler and the heavy, tumbling of
the logs that fed it; the threatening proximity of the mighty, swiftly
flowing river, coursing past only inches below the lower deck
planking; man-eating crocodiles floating in wait for the next meal;
the mammoth bumps and humps and snorts of monstrous
hippos—these were all vivid sights, smells, and sounds never
forgotten by the *Lapsley's* child passengers.

Happy meals, classes, and games shared on the upper deck;
glimpses of tropical wildlife such as a mother elephant taking her
baby to the river for a drink, or graceful herons, screeching parrots,
plummeting fish eagles or snake-necked darters; stifling mosquito
nets, the smothering heat of the tiny cabins at night (especially if
yours happened to be on the landward side); the ominous hordes
of life-threatening insects; the fascination of the rhythmic,
cascading torrent that was the *Lapsley's* spinning stern-wheel; the
interesting walks ashore in the evenings and on Sunday after-
noons—these are remembrances, some exciting and happy, some
uncomfortable or scary, that are still retained from childhood.

Sunday Afternoons Ashore, Special Times

On regular weekdays there were brief afternoon walks through
the forest when the *Lapsley* moored early to load firewood for the
morrow's journey. The wiry, muscular woodcutters jumped into
the shallow water even before the gangplank was extended. They
vanished instantly behind the thick wall of riverside foliage. The
steady ring of their axes could soon be heard in the distance,
coming from various directions.

Parents with children welcomed the chance to let the little ones use up some of that excess energy. But they returned in time to get the children to supper under the big net covering the dining area, then quickly to bed in the cabin by nightfall. What a secure, cozy feeling it always was to be lovingly tucked by your mother into the narrow bunk! The protective mosquito net was stiflingly hot but you knew it kept you safe from the lethal mosquito, as well as other flying insects and "creepy critters."

But Sundays were delightfully different, for the *Lapsley* never traveled on the Lord's Day. All aboard, including the all-important boiler, rested on that day. A full service of worship for both crew and passengers together was held on the upper deck in the morning. After a particularly bountiful meal, everyone took a nap. As soon as the noontide heat subsided, passengers went ashore for long, unhurried walks. On these wonderful excursions parents shared with their children their accumulated knowledge of the distinctive flora and fauna of the fascinating tropical forest or the interesting Bantu village life.

From a river steamer's decks, the Zaire's banks generally give an impression of impenetrable undergrowth. The wide expanse of open water allows sunlight to encourage this luxurious foliage along the shore. Once through that first, apparently forbidding wall of green, the forest is surprisingly free of undergrowth. A vaulted, cathedral-like spaciousness, moist, cool, and windless, inspires a sense of peaceful reverence. Multiple, massive buttressed trunks are the fluted pillars of this natural sanctuary. A beautiful intermeshed ceiling is formed by the sun's rays piercing the spreading crowns of the emergent trees of the overhead canopy. The forest floor has a soft, spongy mat of decomposing vegetation that silences every footfall. Over this mat is a designed carpet of moving patches of sunlight, filtered down through the wind-rumpled branches high above.[140]

On these leisurely Sunday afternoon walks, fathers pointed out to their children the kind of trees from which the long dugout canoes were made and the various kinds of hardwoods and mahoganies that have such beautifully colored, fine-grained woods. Long rattan lianas, attached to the crowns of their host trees by hooked tendrils, offered natural vine swings for the children or a chance to grab on and "play Tarzan." Still another joy of Sunday walks was collecting forest seeds, truly amazing in size, shape, and variety.[141]

Sometimes there were enormous elephant tracks, over which the little ones had to be lifted, or the small dainty tracks of a diminutive forest antelope, the wise little "hero" of much Bantu folklore. High up in the canopy, a troop of chattering *nkima*, redtail monkeys, often demonstrated the use of their bushy tails as directional stabilizers by leaping across amazing distances. Many an African and mission child has happily cherished one of these clown-faced monkeys as a pet!

A comical Hercules beetle might scurry across the path, while the rustle of a colony of forest termites busily at work, is heard among the rotting leaves. Swarms of white butterflies gather to feed here and there on the forest floor. Occasionally one chances to glimpse among the massive trunks the slow, clumsy flight of a grotesque, black-casqued hornbill or hear the continuous trilling and cheeping of a bulbul.[142]

Farther upriver, on long stretches of the Kasai and Sankuru Rivers, instead of endless forests, there are wide expanses of rolling savanna, dotted with wooded copses, framed by distant blue hills. Along certain sections of these rivers are high clay cliffs, the nesting places of great colonies of African gray parrots with their bright red tail feathers. The passing of the swiftly moving paddle wheeler and the sound of its whistle occasioned a wild melee of flapping wings and raucous, frightened screeches, much to the delight of the children.

When the *Lapsley* moored on Sundays at various Kasai villages, Sunday walks included happy visits or services with scattered groups of Christians or joining the children in musical games, laughingly trying to learn their tricky, syncopated mixture of song, dance, and hand clapping. At night, all those aboard went to sleep to the lullaby of distant village drums and marimbas, accompanying a chorus of rich African voices singing in harmonious, pulsating measure.

The heritage of mission children who grew up in the Belgian Congo is a rich one. Those who were fortunate enough to have been there in the 1920s were particularly privileged to have been small, observant passengers on the beloved mission steamer, the *Samuel N. Lapsley.*

Notes

1. Thomas Pakenham, *The Scramble for Africa* (Random House, 1991).

2. Ibid., text inside jacket.

3. Ibid., 13–14.

4. Ibid., 15, 20–22.

5. Ibid., 149.

6. Ibid., 154–55.

7. Ibid., 254.

8. Ibid., 411–12.

9. Ibid., 590–91.

10. T. C. Vinson, *William McCutchan Morrison, Twenty Years in Central Africa* (Richmond, Va.: Presbyterian Committee of Publication, Texarkana, AR-TX, 1921), 51–52.

11. Samuel Hall Chester, *Memories of Four-Score Years* (Richmond, Va.: Presbyterian Committee of Publication, 1934), 169.

12. Pakenham, *The Scramble for Africa*, 594, 600–01 .

13. Ethel Taylor Wharton, *Led in Triumph* (Board of World Missions, Presbyterian Church, U.S., 1952), 72.

14. Vinson, *William McCutchan Morrison, Twenty Years in Central Africa*, 82–83.

15. Ibid., 94.

16. W. M. Morrison, "Some Phases of the Trial of Sheppard and Morrison," *The Kasai Herald* (March 1910): 8–9.

17. Chester, *Memories of Four-Score Years*, 170–76.

18. Letter from Dr. S. H. Chester, Executive Secretary of Committee of Foreign Missions to L. C. Vass, August 11, 1909.

19. Vinson, *William McCutchan Morrison, Twenty Years in Central Africa*, 96.

20. Ibid., 98–99.

21. Ibid., 104.

22. Ibid., 108.

23. Morrison, "Some Phases of the Trial of Sheppard and Morrison," 8–9.

24. Scott's Application to the Executive Committee of Foreign Missions, Presbyterian Church, U.S., November 1905.

25. Ibid.

26. "News Items," *The Kasai Herald* (January 1909): 15.

27. Ibid.

28. Vinson, *William McCutchan Morrison, Twenty Years in Central Africa*, 90–91.

29. L. C. Vass letter to S. H. Chester, July 20, 1909.

30. *American Presbyterian Congo Mission Meeting Minutes*, May 26, 1909.

31. Ibid.

32. W. B. Scott's letter to L. C. Vass, May 26, 1909.

33. *The Kasai Herald* (March 1, 1910): 2.

34. L. C. Vass, "Annual Letter to the Committee," *The Kasai Herald* (January 1, 1909).

35. *The Kasai Herald* (March 1, 1910): 2.

36. *The Kasai Herald* (January, 1910): 3.

37. W. B. Scott letter to L. C. Vass, July 26, 1910.

38. Ibid.

39. *Minutes of Executive Committee of Foreign Missions of the Presbyterian Church, U.S.*, September 6, 1910.

40. *American Presbyterian Congo Mission Meeting Minutes*, November 12, 1910.

41. *The Kasai Herald* (January 1911): 2.

42. Ibid.

43. Ibid.

44. Rachel Boyd Scott, "From Scotland to the Congo," *The Missionary Survey* (April 1912): 421.

45. Ibid.

46. Althea Brown Edmiston, *The Missionary Survey* (April 1912): 421.

47. W. B. Scott, "Our Congo Steamer, The *Lapsley*," *The Missionary Survey* (May 1912): 506–07.

48. "The *Lapsley* Chartered," *The Missionary Survey* (September 1912): 833.

49. Ibid.

50. C. L. Crane, "Notes from Luebo," *The Missionary Survey* (January 1913): 228.

51. Arch C. McKinnon, *Kapitene of the Congo Steamship Lapsley* (Boston: The Christopher Publishing House), 9–11.

52. Ibid., 11.

53. Ibid., 14, 16.

54. Ibid., 19–20.

55. Ibid., 21–22.

56. Ibid., 24–25.

57. "Steamboat Department," *The Kasai Herald* (April 1913).

58. "Steamer Department," *The Kasai Herald* (July 14, 1913): 3.

59. McKinnon, *Kapitene of the Congo Steamship*, 35–37.

60. C. L. Crane, "Annual Meeting of the Congo Mission," *The Missionary Survey* (May 1913): 510–11.

61. Pakenham, *The Scramble for Africa*, 437.

62. R. D. Bedinger, "A Trip to Lusambo," *The Kasai Herald* (January 1913): 8–11.

63. A. C. McKinnon, "Lusambo Station," *The Missionary Survey* (April 1914): 291–93.

64. "Steamer Department: Wood Posts," *Ad Interim Committee Minutes, American Presbyterian Congo Mission*, May 6, 1913.

65. Ibid., "Steamer Rules."

66. "Steamer Department," *American Presbyterian Congo Mission Meeting Minutes*, January 21, 1914, items 1–6.

67. Vinson, *William McCutchan Morrison, Twenty Years in Central Africa*, 131.

68. Ibid., 132.

69. Ibid., 132–33.

70. McKinnon, *Kapitene of the Congo Steamship*, 23.

71. W. B. Weaver, *Thirty-Five Years in the Congo*, (Chicago, Il.: Congo Inland Mission, 1945), 179–103.

72. Ibid.

73. McKinnon, *Kapitene of the Congo Steamship*, 23.

74. "Steamer Department: Steamer Trips," *The Kasai Herald* (April 1, 1913).

75. *American Presbyterian Congo Mission Minutes,* January 9, 1914, 9.

76. W. R. Lambuth, "The Call of Africa," Brochure, Board of World Missions, Methodist Episcopal Church, South, Nashville, Tn., 4–5.

77. Ann L. Ashmore, *The Call of the Congo* (Nashville: Parthenon Press, 1958), 20–21.

78. Mary Dabney, *Light in Darkness* (Bedinger missionary record, 1971), 52–53.

79. Ibid., 53.

80. Ibid.

81. Vinson, *William McCutchan Morrison*, 134.

82. McKinnon, *Kapitene of the Congo Steamship*, 47.

83. Roy Cleveland, family letter dated February 1914.

84. D. L. Mumpower, "What Presbyterians Have Done for Methodists," *The Missionary Survey* (July 1914): 530–32.

85. Mary Dabney, *Light in Darkness*, 55.

86. Ibid.

87. Mumpower, *The Missionary Survey* (July 1914): 532.

88. Mrs. R. F. Cleveland, "Introducing Congo Christians: Baba Malundola, A Congo Saint," *The Presbyterian Survey* (February 1954): 30.

89. Ibid.

90. Mumpower, *The Missionary Survey* (July 1914): 532.

91. Cecilia Irvine, *The Church of Christ in Zaire, A Handbook of Protestant Churches, Missions and Communities, 1878–1978* (Indianapolis, In.: Christian Church Services, Inc., (Disciples of Christ), 1978), 104–05.

92. McKinnon, *Kapitene of the Congo Steamship*, 64–67.

93. Irvine, *The Church of Christ in Zaire*, 104–05.

94. *Official Records of the Board of Foreign Missions of the Presbyterian Church, U.S.*, Mr. and Mrs. J. T. Daumery.

95. Annual Report of the American Presbyterian Congo Mission, *The Kasai Herald*, 5.

96. "Foreign Missions: Africa," *The Missionary Survey* (April 1915): 1.

97. McKinnon, *Kapitene of the Congo Steamship*, 49–52

98. Ibid., 95.

99. W. M. Morrison and T. C. Vinson, "Notes and Comments," *The Kasai Herald* (November 1915): 1.

100. McKinnon, *Kapitene of the Congo Steamship*, 6–13.

101. Ibid.

102. Winifred K. Vass, *Doctor Not Afraid* (Austin, Tx.: Nortex Press, 1986), 106.

103. McKinnon, *Kapitene of the Congo Steamship*, 63.

104. "Annual Report of the American Presbyterian Congo Mission," *The Missionary Survey* (April 1918): 239.

105. Letter in French from Belgian Congo Territorial Commissioner to the Legal Representative of the American Presbyterian Congo Mission, June 6, 1916.

106. Louise Seymour Houghton, *Handbook of French and Belgian Protestantism* (Federal Council of Churches of Christ in America, 1919), 72.

107. Vass, *Doctor Not Afraid*, 147–48.

108. Vinson, *William McCutchan Morrison*, 141–43.

109. Mary Dabney, *Light in Darkness*, 118–19.

110. Letter written aboard the *Lapsley* by Plumer Smith to "Dear Friends," September 3–4, 1923.

111. *American Presbyterian Congo Mission Meeting Minutes*, November 29–December 14, 1921, items 4, 56, 76, no. 4.

112. *American Presbyterian Congo Mission Meeting Minutes*, October 12, 1925, item no. 15 (Committee of the Whole).

113. *Minutes of the Executive Committee of Foreign Missions, Presbyterian Church, U.S.*, April 1929.

114. *Official Records of the Executive Committee of Foreign Missions, Presbyterian Church, U.S.*, Rev. and Mrs. S. H. Wilds.

115. *American Presbyterian Congo Mission Meeting Minutes*, October 23, 1923, item 15.

116. J. Hershey Longenecker, *Memories of Congo* (Johnson City, Tn.: Royal Publishers, Inc., 1964), 78.

117. *American Presbyterian Congo Mission Meeting Minutes,* Summary of 1928–1929 Statistics, 65.

118. Andre Lederer, *Histoire de la Navigation au Congo,* Musée Royal de l'Afrique Centrale, Teruvuren, Belgique, Annales, Serie IN-8, Sciences Historiques, no. 2 (1965), 75, 145, 147.

119. Ibid., 145.

120. Ann L. Ashmore, *The Call of the Congo,* 83–84.

121. Mrs. S. H. Wilds, "On the Steamer *Lapsley,*" *Lumu lua Bena Kasai* (October 1929): 1.

122. S. H. Wilds's Reminiscences, (taped at Luebo, 1954).

123. Plumer Smith, letter to "Dear Friends," November 26, 1924.

124. Letter from Anne Wilds McLean to Winifred K. Vass, May 31, 1992.

125. *Official Records of the Board of Foreign Missions, Presbyterian Church, U.S.,* Mr. and Mrs. J. F. Watt.

126. *Minutes of the Executive Committee of Foreign Missions, Presbyterian Church, U.S.,* "Missionary Department," June 1925.

127. Missionary Correspondence Department letter from Mrs. Franklin Watt November 1926.

128. Letter from Mrs. Franklin Watt to Winifred K. Vass, July 20, 1992.

129. J. F. Watt, "Come with Me on the *Lapsley,*" *The Presbyterian Survey* (April 1930): 227–29.

130. Bessie S. Martin, "Arrival of Missionaries," *The Kasai Herald* (January 1913): 8.

131. *The Missionary Survey* (January 1914): 35; and *The Kasai Herald* (January, 1915): 8.

132. Louise Crane, "Ku Mputu," excerpt from unpublished book about her parents, Dr. and Mrs. Charles LaCoste Crane, 58.

133. William J. Anderson, "A Trip on the *Lapsley,*" *The Missionary Survey* (September 1922): 681–82.

134. Letter from "Sanky" Stegall Norwood to Winifred K. Vass, May 28, 1992.

135. Letter from Anne Boyd Cleveland Crane to Winifred K. Vass, June 23, 1992.

136. Letter from Ruth Smith Gilmer to Winifred K. Vass, August 8, 1992.

137. Letter from Charles McKee to Winifred K. Vass, July 6, 1992.

138. Letter from Dorothy Longenecker Hopper to Winifred K. Vass, May 27, 1992.

139. Letter from John Knox Miller to Winifred K. Vass, June 3, 1992.

140. Edward S. Ayensu, *Jungles* (New York: Crown Publishers, Inc., 1980), 177–79.

141. H. F. Macmillan, *Tropical Planting and Gardening* (London: Macmillan and Company, Ltd., 1949), 126–27.

142. W. A. Fairbairn, *Some Common Birds of West Africa* (London: The Highway Press, 1933), 44–45, 47, 50, 54, 76.

Part V

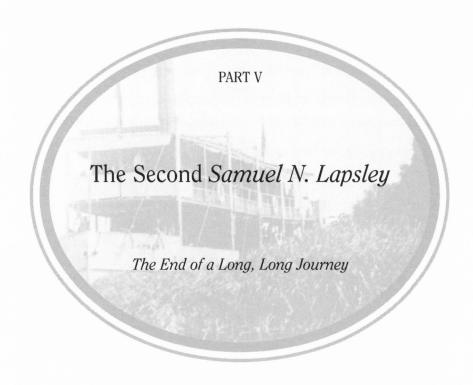

PART V

The Second *Samuel N. Lapsley*

The End of a Long, Long Journey

The Many Roles of a Versatile Veteran

THE *SAMUEL N. LAPSLEY* WAS AN ACTIVE PARTICIPANT IN the high drama of the years of King Leopold II's Congo Free State. The stern-wheeler functioned as a diplomatic courier when it carried British Consul Thesiger upriver to investigate the ghastly results of the greedy exploitation of the Congo's rubber and ivory resources. It was Thesiger's report to the British Parliament that helped open up the international debate that finally removed the Free State from the king's grasp and made it a Belgian colony. On all its trips, the *Lapsley* was a mail steamer, bringing anticipated letters, news, fresh reading material, and packages from loved ones far away.

The steamer was also a navigational record office, for ship's logs were carefully kept, according to Belgian shipping requirements.

In addition, it was a traveling hotel with extremely cozy accommodations and delicious meals served either in the dining salon or on deck. As on giant ocean liners, mealtime was always announced by the mellow tones of musical chimes, struck with a felt-tipped mallet.

Heavy crates, barrels, and boxes stacked in the hold and on the deck indicated that the mission steamer was a much-needed essential cargo transport.

Baluba Mingi—"Many Baluba" was the name used for the *Lapsley* by the native peoples up and down the river. An entire Baluba village made up of crew members, their wives and children, plus assorted chickens and goats camped on the lower deck, all maintaining the regular activities of daily village life. Occasionally the crew maintained a floating butcher's shop.

The upper deck was often a barber shop as laughing passengers, often inexperienced haircutters, gave each other unexpected, new-styling haircuts.

Sometimes the *Lapsley* was a hospital ship, carrying gravely ill missionaries downriver to return to the homeland. At the signal of a white flag anywhere along the riverbanks, the steamer always stopped to render any possible medical assistance or bury the dead.

The stern-wheeler was also a language school, as new missionaries sat with native crew members, practicing the unfamiliar words, sounds, and intonations. Passengers' children sometimes studied their home-schooling textbooks under their mother's direction. The *Lapsley's* upper deck was a breeze-cooled, scenic classroom.

For Captain Franklin Watt and his bride, Georgia McKay, the *Lapsley* was a honeymoon cruiser, for they took over the captaincy only one week after they were married in 1925.

The upper deck provided a nursery or playground for both the captain's and passengers' children, and the sturdy stanchions provided gymnastic equipment. There was room for jumping rope, jacks, or hopscotch. There was always the fun of watching the powerful paddle wheel at the stern.

Excited passengers soon discovered that the *Lapsley* was a moving wildlife observation station. Hours were spent leaning over the railings exclaiming over frantic antics of crocodiles, monkeys, hippos, elephants, or tropical river birds reacting to the ship's passing.

Missionaries of many different societies were warmly welcomed aboard the *Lapsley*. The steamer's uniquely ecumenical role was particularly apparent in the passenger and transport services rendered both to the Congo Inland Mission (Mennonite) and the Methodist Episcopal Congo Mission during the initial stages of their establishment.

Above all, the *Samuel N. Lapsley* was a floating church. Each weekday, a brief morning worship was held on the lower deck before the moorings were loosed and the anchor chain drawn in to release the steamer for the day's journey ahead. On Sundays the mission steamer, crew, and passengers rested, first worshiping together in a full church service, then enjoying a leisurely Sunday dinner, followed by a long nap or walk through the towering trees, often growing right up to the steamer's landing place. If there was a village where the *Lapsley* had tied up over the Sabbath, a service was also held there, and friendly visits were made with the residents. At village after village up and down the river, small groups of Christian believers gathered, having first heard the Good News of Jesus Christ through the presence of the steamer on their shore.

The Decision To Sell the *Lapsley*

Requests to buy the mission steamer had been coming in from possible buyers for a number of years. For instance, a letter dated February 25, 1920, from a group of Lusambo merchants, written in French, pleaded:

> As you know, Lusambo is simply gorged these days with huge quantities of local products awaiting shipment downriver.

> The navigational provisions for shipment by the State are prac-
> tically non-existent. We beg you to sell us the *Lapsley* or at least
> lease it for several round trips. We promise you more than
> adequate remuneration![1]

In November 1926, Mrs. Franklin Watt, wife of the captain,
wrote to her home church, "Our *Lapsley* has been running now for
twenty-one years and is still in such good condition that several
offers have been made for her by commercial enterprises."[2]

There were a number of determining factors in the decision to
sell the mission stern-wheeler. One very important reason was the
Belgian Congo developed its own monetary system. From 1891,
when the mission was founded, up into the 1920s, "barter goods"
were the only means of making purchases. Necessary supplies
were bought by trading with salt, cowrie shells, beads, blankets, or
cloth. All mission salaries were paid in such commodities. Needed
materials purchased for construction of hospitals, schools, and
residences and also for station operation were being transported
by the *Lapsley*.

In February 1928, the American Presbyterian Congo Mission
voted to eliminate the system of barter purchase as mission policy
for the following reasons:

> Benefits derived from handling barter goods are rapidly
> disappearing on account of changing conditions in the
> Belgian Congo. So many trading companies are being estab-
> lished that the Congolese who work for us are no longer
> dependent on us for these goods. The handling of barter
> goods is increasingly placing the Mission in the same cate-
> gory as traders. The local people feel that we are profiting
> financially. We will never have a more propitious time than
> the present to eliminate this as a policy of the Mission.[3]

This action directly affected the *Lapsley*, for most of the upriver
cargo had for years been barter goods items.

The 1929 mission meeting was deeply concerned with the
continued use of the *Lapsley* itself. Excellent passenger accommodations at less expense were now available on Belgian commercial

riverboat lines. These could be obtained promptly and entailed no prolonged wait at either end of a journey, as had been the case with only one steamer in use.

Also, the *Lapsley* had never been insured, unlike all competing company boats. With age and use the stern-wheeler was in increasing need of repair. Funds for such were simply not available to the mission during the Great Depression.[4] For all these reasons, the mission formally approved the sale of the *Samuel N. Lapsley* on May 3, 1930.[5]

The final price, 175,000 Belgian francs, was set and promptly paid by a Mr. Bracone.[6] This amount ($4,928.50) was set aside as a nucleus for a $20,000 fund for constructing the Lapsley Memorial Hospital at Bulape.[7] This hospital, under the direction of the Presbyterian Church of Zaire, is staffed with trained Zairien medical personnel.[8]

It is fitting that the *Lapsley's* ministry of faithful, compassionate service still lives on in Zaire today in the hospital that bears that name.

"God's Steamer" Called to Secular Duty

Many tearful visits were paid to the beloved paddle wheeler as it awaited the arrival of its new owners. Crew members, who had lived for weeks on end on her decks, missionaries from each of the mission's stations, and the children of the mission especially grieved over her imminent departure.

Captain Wilds arranged to "steam up" the boiler one more time and take a large group on one last short trip down the Lulua River and back. The Alex Shive and Plumer Smith families took a picnic supper to the familiar site at the foot of Luebo hill, which had been the steamer's "home base" for so many years, and then told their friend a fond farewell.[9]

Dr. Eugene Kellersberger took his teenage daughter, Winifred, on board to see the cabin in which she had slept under the hot mosquito netting as a small child. She had never forgotten watching the huge head of a hippo erupt with a thundering splash from right under the ship, where she had stood on the deck.

For the next eighteen years the *Lapsley* was used by a company working on the Upper Congo waterways. Only an occasional glimpse of the former mission steamer would be caught by those who recognized the familiar shape and never-to-be-forgotten two-toned whistle.

Two of these occasions were in 1939. Dr. John Knox Miller recalls:

> When we were going downriver on the *Luxembourg* in 1939, one evening just at dusk we tied up for wood. Another steamer came in from downriver and tied up just in front of us. My Dad and the other missionaries at once recognized it as the *Lapsley*. It belonged at that time to OTRACO. (Office of Exploitation of Colonial Transport.)[10]

The Plumer Smith family also saw the former mission steamer. Mrs. John B. Gilmer (Ruth Smith) describes what happened:

> In 1939, we sighted the *Lapsley* again. My father had evidently been expecting to see it, for he pointed it out to us from the deck of the *Luxembourg* as we churned downriver. The *Lapsley* was loaded with bulging sacks and riding low in the water. It looked dingy and unkempt, but was sturdily doing a big job. My sister, Bettie Anne, remembers that it had the Greek name of *Olga*. The *Luxembourg* tooted a salute, as we passed the slower ship. Then, once again came that distinctive whistle that had so many times brought joyous, singing crowds down to the shore at Luebo.[11]

When Lachlan Vass III was traveling downriver in 1945 on the ex-Mississippi riverboat, *Kigoma*, the captain recognized the name and was most excited to meet the son of the *Lapsley's* assembler and captain. He exclaimed, "That's the finest steamer on the entire Congo River system! When it was up for sale, I did my level best to buy it myself!"

In 1948, the former mission steamer again changed owners. She was bought by a merchant to be a floating store and to handle

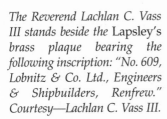

The Reverend Lachlan C. Vass III stands beside the Lapsley's *brass plaque bearing the following inscription: "No. 609, Lobnitz & Co. Ltd., Engineers & Shipbuilders, Renfrew." Courtesy—Lachlan C. Vass III.*

transport between Port Francqui and Luebo. The name, *Semois,* was painted across her bridge. Again, the familiar whistle was heard from far down the river, as she made occasional trips back to the old "home base," once more carrying transport for the American Presbyterian Congo Mission.

On one of these visits to Luebo, the Vass family, living there, went aboard and took pictures of Captain Vass's grandchildren in the wheelhouse of his beloved vessel and of them standing on the Lulua riverbank beside it.

The Search for a "Presbyterian Artifact"

Inquiries into the location of the retired *Lapsley* were made during the 1960s, while a Zaire mission movie called "Tale of Two Rivers" was being filmed for the Presbyterian Church. At that time a Congolese riverboat captain showed Dr. John Knox Miller a large illustrated navigational history book, containing information on each of the Belgian Congo government steamers. The *Lapsley* was pictured in this volume, together with the date it had been retired from government service many years earlier. Dr. Miller does not remember the date. The Congolese captain thought that the former mission steamer was probably tied up in the "ship boneyard" at Limete, Kinshasa.[12]

Julia Lake Vass (left) and Winifred Vass, holding "Lilibet," watch cargo brought upriver on the Semois *being loaded onto trucks. Courtesy—Lachlan C. Vass III.*

While assigned to Kinshasa from 1962–1965, the Reverend David Miller went with a friend to search the shipyard area of the city. There they found the *Lapsley's* hull still afloat; all superstructure had been removed. So carefully assembled had been that hull with red hot rivets under Captain Vass's careful direction that it was still strong and watertight. When last seen, it was being used as a floating dock for the use of incoming riverboats with cargo to unload. Even the "skeleton" of that blessed ship was still useful!

In 1969 Dr. Kenneth J. Foreman Jr. became executive director of the Historical Foundation of the Presbyterian and Reformed Churches. Since childhood he had been much taken with the admiralty model of the *Lapsley* which, with Captain Vass's cap and the ship's bell, is on prominent display in that historical agency. As executive director, he wanted to discover if the venerable steamer were still afloat.

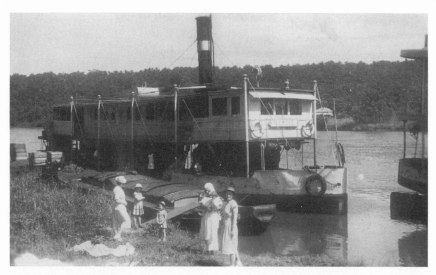

The Semois, *originally the* Samuel N. Lapsley, *unloads cargo from barges in tow. On the bank at Luebo, left to right, are Emily Boehler, Edna Vass, Julia Lake Vass, Baba Konkolongo Lebeka holding "Lilibet" and Winifred Vass. Courtesy—Lachlan C. Vass III.*

He had the dream of locating her, having her taken apart, as once she had been by her makers on Clydeside, crated up once more, and shipped to the Montreat Conference Center in western North Carolina. He was certain that by following the model, which can still be seen today at what is now the Department of History of the Presbyterian Church (U.S.A.), Montreat, the original hull could be reassembled and floated on Lake Susan; and, with upper works restored, the resurrected *Lapsley* could then become both a striking historical shrine and memorable guest quarters for the instruction and enjoyment of the denomination's members. Such a living reminder of Presbyterian mission work in Central Africa could bring home to thousands each year a vivid sense of their Church's remarkable missionary heritage.

During the course of Dr. Foreman's inquiries, a high officer of the Virginia National Guard learned of the project and volunteered to arrange for the capacious cargo planes of the Guard's Air Wing to ferry the dismantled hull from Kinshasa to the nearby Asheville

Edna Vass (right) stands where her grandfather, Captain Vass, so often stood. Luebo educational missionary, Emily Boehler, Julia Lake, and baby "Lilibet" Vass also enjoy exploring the former Lapsley's *wheelhouse (April 1948). Courtesy—Lachlan C. Vass III.*

airport—on training flights, free of charge.

But this was not to be. A letter to Dr. John Pritchard from J. Nzeke of OTRACO, written from former Leopoldville, brought the news that "the boat no longer exists."[13] Later investigations on the Zaire riverbank by a missionary who had seen it there in earlier days confirmed the fact that no trace of the vessel, not even the hull which had been serving as a floating dock, was now left afloat.[14]

Ave Atque Vale* for a Valiant Vessel
*"Hail and Farewell!" (Hello and Goodbye!)

Perhaps it is even more fitting that all which used to be the *Samuel N. Lapsley* remains near the river and among the people for whom the steamer was fabricated to serve.

Here and there in Kinshasa, that huge capital city of over three million people (no longer called by the colonial name of "Leopoldville"), a worn brass knob opens the door to a Zairien house. A length of polished teakwood board forms part of a home-made table. Now and again some of the small copper basins which, like those on great ocean liners, were to be found between the bunks in each cabin, are today used to dry peanuts in the sun! And a strong, iron stanchion that supported the *Lapsley's* upper-deck canopy now provides a corner support for a grass-roofed house. Finding them may be difficult, but in a land where useful things which endure are prized, we can be sure that these and many other parts of the old stern-wheeler are still treasured and useful.

If ever a man-made combination of manufactured materials became a living personality, it was the *Samuel N. Lapsley*! If ever such a product of human skill and design was an expression of the love of the Eternal God for the people of his creation, it was the *Lapsley*! The willing servant-spirit of the American Presbyterian Congo Mission's beloved steamboat surely still dwells upon the Zaire River.

At any moment now, from behind a forested bend, that unique, melodious whistle will sound. The strong, sturdy prow will steam smoothly into view, cleanly parting the brown waters before it. Proudly, the *Samuel N. Lapsley* will pass by, spray-drenched paddle wheel rhythmically churning, leaving a widening wedge of foaming wake upon the restless brooding surface of that great river on which so long and well she served her Master.

Notes

1. Letter from Ramalkete Figuiredre to director of the Mission, Luebo, Lusambo, February 25, 1920.

2. Missionary correspondence letter of Georgia McKay Watt, Presbyterian Church, U.S., November 1926.

3. *Minutes of the Executive Committee of Foreign Missions, Presbyterian Church, U.S.,* February 1928, regarding action of American Presbyterian Congo Mission.

4. "Advantages and Disadvantages of Selling the *Lapsley*," *American Presbyterian Congo Mission Meeting Minutes*, October 18, 1929.

5. American Presbyterian Congo Mission Ad Interim Committee meeting, May 3, 1930.

6. "Final Price Set for Sale of the *Lapsley*," *American Presbyterian Congo Mission Meeting*, October 1932, items 32–46.

7. "Approval of $4,900 from Sale of *Lapsley* for Bulape Hospital," *Executive Committee of Foreign Missions Meeting*, December 1935.

8. "Approval of Use of *Lapsley* Sale Fund," for building the Lapsley Memorial Hospital at Bulape, *American Presbyterian Congo Mission Meeting*, October 1934, items 34–409.

9. Ruth Smith Gilmer's letter to Winifred K. Vass, August 8, 1992.

10. John Knox Miller's letter to Winifred K. Vass, June 3, 1992.

11. Gilmer letter to Vass, August 8, 1992.

12. Miller letter to Vass, June 3, 1992.

13. William Bynum's letter to Winifred K. Vass, regarding Kenneth J. Foreman Jr., files at Department of History, PCUSA, Montreat, North Carolina.

14. Kenneth J. Foreman Jr., Files at Department of History, PCUSA, Montreat, North Carolina.

Index

231

Index